ogy
A Beginner's Guide

"A superb guide, one of the very few to combine biological and social approaches."

Dr David Shankland - Director of the
Royal Anthropological Institute

"An excellent place to start discovering the range and depth of anthropological enquiry."

Professor Robert A. Foley - Director of the
Leverhulme Centre for Human Evolutionary Studies,
University of Cambridge

"A wonderfully accessible introduction, with a clear focus on the needs of students first coming to the field."

Dr Faye Healey-Clough - Anthropology lecturer,
Gloucestershire College, UK

ONEWORLD BEGINNER'S GUIDES combine an original, inventive, and engaging approach with expert analysis on subjects ranging from art and history to religion and politics, and everything in-between. Innovative and affordable, books in the series are perfect for anyone curious about the way the world works and the big ideas of our time.

aesthetics
africa
american politics
anarchism
animal behaviour
anthropology
anti-capitalism
aquinas
art
artificial intelligence
the bahai faith
the beat generation
the bible
biodiversity
bioterror & biowarfare
the brain
british politics
the Buddha
cancer
censorship
christianity
civil liberties
classical music
climate change
cloning
cold war
conservation
crimes against humanity
criminal psychology
critical thinking
daoism
democracy
descartes
dewey

dyslexia
energy
the enlightenment
engineering
epistemology
european union
evolution
evolutionary psychology
existentialism
fair trade
feminism
forensic science
french literature
french revolution
genetics
global terrorism
hinduism
history of science
homer
humanism
huxley
iran
islamic philosophy
islamic veil
journalism
judaism
lacan
life in the universe
literary theory
machiavelli
mafia & organized crime
magic
marx
medieval philosophy

middle east
modern slavery
NATO
the new testament
nietzsche
the northern ireland conflict
nutrition
oil
opera
the palestine–israeli conflict
particle physics
paul
philosophy
philosophy of mind
philosophy of religion
philosophy of science
planet earth
postmodernism
psychology
quantum physics
the qur'an
racism
reductionism
religion
renaissance art
the russian revolution
shakespeare
the small arms trade
sufism
the torah
united nations
volcanoes

Beginners
GUIDES

Anthropology
A Beginner's Guide

Joy Hendry and Simon Underdown

ONEWORLD

A Oneworld Paperback Original

Published by Oneworld Publications 2012
Reprinted 2013

Copyright © Joy Hendry and Simon Underdown 2012

The moral right of Joy Hendry and Simon Underdown to be identified
as the Authors of this work has been asserted by them in accordance with
the Copyright, Designs and Patents Act 1988

ISBN 978-1-85168-930-9
eBook 978-1-78074-117-8

Typeset by Cenveo Publisher Services, Bangalore, India
Cover design by vaguelymemorable.com

Printed and bound in Denmark by Nørhaven A/S

Oneworld Publications
10 Bloomsbury Street
London WC1B 3SR
England

Contents

Acknowledgements

Anthropology, the study of humankind in all its diversity, is an exciting subject that should be open and available to anyone, and we are grateful to Marsha Filion and Juliet Mabey at Oneworld for offering us the opportunity to bring our field to the wide public audience we think it deserves. We would also like to thank Fiona Slater and Ruth Deary for negotiating the practical details of its production.

This opening up of the discipline is a venture close to our hearts. As it happens, when we were invited to write this book we were already involved in a related venture, as part of the Education Committee of the Royal Anthropological Institute (RAI) in London, which was tasked with devising ways to bring anthropology to pre-university students, as well as the public at large. Our work on the book thus developed alongside the syllabus for the Advanced-level Certificate of Education in England, which reflected the hard work of chair, Brian Street, and the director of the RAI at the time, Hilary Callan. We would therefore like to thank them and our fellow committee members for their various contributions to this book, notably Marzia Balzani, Paul Basu, David Bennett, Laura Bishop, Stephanie Bunn, Barry Dufour, Luke Freeman, Judith Okely, Peggy Froerer, Bonnie Vandesteeg and Rob Webb, as well as Gemma Jones and Nafisa Fera, who were the education officers during the period, and David Shankland who succeeded Hilary Callan as Director of the RAI in 2010.

For other comments on aspects of the text at various stages of its production, we would like to thank Andrew and Leslie Carter, Chris Dunabin, Rob Foley, Martin and Sofia Gellner, Sandy Hendry, Emily Hendry, Kate Hill, William Kay, Zoe Lake Thomas, Jenny McKenna, Nancy Priston, Mary Patterson, Charles Tyson Taylor and Jemma Underdown.

Introduction

Anthropology is a twenty-first century subject with roots as old as human history. As long as people have wondered where they come from, and speculated about the behaviour of neighbours brought up differently to themselves, they have been thinking anthropologically. For several decades, we have been able to watch people from all sorts of backgrounds on television, but we also often find ourselves beside them, for instance, in school or at work. Some may have travelled from afar, but many have grown up in the same towns and cities we share. We may practise different rites and ceremonies, eat different food at home, and possibly even speak different languages. We may or may not look like one another, though we probably share a local way of speaking with those who live nearby. Yet our families and our backgrounds are intriguingly different.

It is only in the decades spanning the opening of the new millennium that it has become possible through the internet to find out instantly about people who live at opposite ends of the earth, to chase up our common features and to marvel at our continuing diversity. Independent of books and teachers, we can track ideas about our evolutionary origins through time, investigate our relationships with the environment, and, if we have the language, we can communicate freely with people whose elders – parents, grandparents and so forth – think quite differently from our own. In all these ways we are already beginning to be anthropologists, for this is essentially where anthropology begins.

Those of us living in this new world thus have an advantage over our elders and ancestors in the access we have to anthropological knowledge, the familiarity we may have with long-distance travel, and the products of multinational companies. However, this book will introduce some of the values that those same elders and ancestors may have for us in a kind of learning that goes beyond the internet. It will suggest ways in which you can draw on your valuable inside knowledge to do anthropology yourself, perhaps by talking to some of those elders, by sharing your own particular worlds with friends, or by hunting for curious objects you can hold in your hands, and examine for clues of former lives. It will offer hints to pushing back further through time, from investigating your family ancestry to suggestions about the biological heritage you and your friends share as human beings.

Some history of the field

Anthropology did not always have such a positive image, and not everybody yet regards anthropology as highly as we, the authors, do, so we will give you a little history to set a context for this new book about the subject. The academic discipline of anthropology was born along with other sciences and social sciences more than a hundred years ago, and it retains links and similarities with some of its fellow offspring of previous eras of European thought. Until the middle of the nineteenth century, scholars who thought about the evolution and behaviour of human beings and their communities were generally known as natural philosophers. However, as European thinking flourished during the later part of that period now described as the Enlightenment, they began to focus their interests on more specific fields. Each of the major sciences adopted their now well-known names like physics, chemistry and biology. New disciplines were devised to examine a concept called society, or the organization of human beings, which one of our intellectual ancestors, Herbert Spencer, argued might obey the same laws as biological organisms.

The role that European anthropologists played at this time was to travel to distant lands, and make studies of the biological characteristics, languages, and social lives of groups of people whose lands had been 'discovered' by explorers. When these were followed by colonizers, anthropologists were asked to help, and as the whole business of colonization has come in for criticism, so has anthropology. The people who were the focus of those early anthropological studies were described as 'primitive', largely because they lacked the technology which was growing at that time in the industrializing nations, and even 'savage', because they tried to resist these invasions of their lands. Native Americans and Australian Aboriginal people are particularly well-known examples of this, although many of those who settled in their lands are at last realizing the wisdom of the people whose lives and cultures they almost destroyed.

Some anthropologists, even in these early times, noticed the complexity of thought that lay behind the apparently strange behaviour of these peoples, and as they spent more time living with them and learning their languages, they discerned ways of thinking that were as logical and sophisticated as their own, but simply very different. Unfortunately, others used studies of Indigenous peoples to rank societies on a scale according to levels of civilization they thought each society had attained. Inevitably, all such scales placed contemporary nineteenth-century Europeans and their colonial descendants firmly at the top of the league table. They were used to justify the policies of assimilation and even elimination applied by 'strong' nations spreading around the world, invading and colonizing the lands of those they perceived as inferior.

An important influence at the time was the writing of Charles Darwin, whose theories of evolution form the basis of a branch of anthropology now called biological, concerned with the origin and development of the human species. Spencer's ideas about society, following some of the same rules as biological organisms, fuelled a general misunderstanding that ideas of evolution could also be applied to social groups, which underpinned the rankings mentioned above. Within the new nations that were formed in places like the Americas, anthropology also included 'culture' as a theme to study, notably the material culture – houses, garments, art, tools, and weapons – that they expected to disappear as the lifestyle of the colonizers was imposed around them. They perhaps had in mind the phrase 'survival of the fittest', now attributed to Darwin, but actually first written by Spencer, and they set out to 'salvage' material they found. Linguistic anthropology did the same with language.

Descendants of these colonized peoples did, as expected, have their lives completely transformed. However, many of them have passed down aspects of their distinctive identities, and now that they have acquired all the same technological skills as their invaders, they often express an understandable resentment about that former imposed system of (mis)classification. Anthropologists associated with the early biological studies – skull measuring, collecting of the bones of the dead, and theories about human evolution which also became confused with those of technological development – have been particularly attacked. Yet in the late twentieth and twenty-first centuries, biological anthropology has undergone a major transformation, which has done much to dispel the notions of its more misguided forebears. The work of fossil analysis and advances in the understanding of DNA has brought entirely new knowledge of our common evolutionary heritage. We can now, for instance, question the validity of the biological concept of 'race' previously used to make hard-and-fast distinctions between present-day human groups.

At the same time, other scholars – known as social, cultural, or linguistic anthropologists – concentrate on describing and comparing the distinctive features of contemporary and recent human societies. Following the work of a founding scholar named Bronisław Malinowski, who was forced through war in his own country to spend several years in the Trobriand Islands and was thus able to illustrate how logical and scientific the behaviour of the Islanders was, anthropologists have built up the distinctive method of study now known as participant observation that requires them also to spend at least a year in their chosen research location. However, some of those same people who were studied by foreign anthropologists in the past now prefer to make studies of themselves, to assert their new-found skills, to argue for the value of the knowledge and abilities their people independently acquired, and to shake off a past era which deemed them 'inferior'.

Anthropology today

So what is the scope of the new anthropology we present in this book? How can it shake off its sometimes murky past? First, the knowledge that has been acquired through the short- and long-term work of many of our anthropological predecessors now constitutes a unique subject for study, different both from the other disciplines like sociology and biology that grew out of the nineteenth-century divisions, as well as from the findings of Indigenous scholars working with their own peoples. No other field can draw on such a wealth of resources about the possibilities for human difference, at the same time as displaying clearly our common humanity. Those carefully collected details of linguistic and social meaning, alongside material culture and human remains now stored in museums, may still sometimes upset the people whose ancestors they catalogued, but it also often remains the best record of their lives. Second, those of us who do the studying understand the need to make a conscientious effort to suspend prejudice, and to cultivate a respect for the different ways of thinking and behaviour we encounter. This offers a practical role for the discipline of anthropology to help with communicating and sharing ideas between peoples of different origins. If our thoughts are curious, rather than confrontational, and they form study rather than a strategy for conflict or exploitation, they not only add to the body of shared knowledge that anthropology has already acquired, but they can also be used to make the world a safer place. For example, advising some of our best-known politicians before they decided to invade and reorganize, according to Western values, the lands of people who live by different codes. Anthropological understanding is not so powerful that it will allow us to avoid all wars and disagreements in the future. People will find plenty of other reasons to fight. But anthropological learning will at least equip you to recognize (for instance) that behaviours which one group may dismiss as 'backwardness' or even 'fanaticism' constitute strategies of defence and protection in the eyes of another.

Interestingly, the diversity in the range of social and cultural traits that make up the human world is not mirrored at the biological level. In this book, we will learn that our species, known as *Homo sapiens* – the name we gave ourselves, which somewhat arrogantly means 'wise man'– is remarkable for its close genetic unity and shared evolutionary history. We presently think that all living humans today can trace their ancestry back to a region of Ethiopia called Omo, where the first *Homo sapiens* lived around two hundred thousand years ago. The outward differences that are often thought to make populations distinct, such as skin colour or body shape, are recent adaptations controlled by a small number of genes, as we shall see in more detail. Like our own families, we are all genetically very similar even though our habits, appearance, and tastes might be quite different. In this book, we will also consider the reasons behind these differences – for example in the way we learn through a whole range of possible languages, which in turn affects the way we communicate.

Learning to share these different worlds, and appreciating just how different they may be, will give you, the reader, skills that could be useful in many walks of life. They should enable you to recognize alternative ways of thinking about the environment in which we live, and to take seriously ideas that some earlier generations ignored.

Another advantage to studying anthropology is that you will learn to understand yourself better, to discover where you came from, and how you evolved as a human being. You will find out what it is that makes us human, and how those characteristics are shared, despite the variety of skin and hair colour, of height and weight, and the extraordinary number of languages and dialects. You will be able to acquire a clearer picture of your cultural make-up, the sources of your own personal identity, and that of the people who came before you and from whom you inherited your ways of thinking about the world. This book is written precisely for people who are interested in working these things out. It is also for students on the threshold of their adult lives, who may be able to make use of this valuable subject to build a new and more secure place for future generations to inhabit.

A tour of the book

The first four chapters of this book set out to illustrate the major underlying themes of *human unity*, demonstrated by the approach of biological anthropology, and *cultural diversity*, which forms the subject matter of social and cultural anthropology. Chapter 1 will start with the biological understanding of our similarities as human beings, by exploring the evolution and development of the biological human body, and how evolutionary pressures have shaped our present form. This will be followed by examples of diverse ways in which different peoples use and understand those same bodies. The differences will be developed in chapters 2 and 3 in considering variations in language, ways of thinking and communicating, and the social relations that groups of people maintain. Chapter 4 will turn to differing social constructions of what may be seen, biologically, as the same environment, and introduce some of the material culture that offers concrete examples of varying human interactions with it.

We will then turn to examine the processes by which human beings become socially defined persons. Chapter 5 will focus on the idea of personhood and present some of the many possibilities for the very notion of *person* within a particular society, and how that person is defined in relation to others. In chapter 6, we will look in detail at *ritual* ways in which such personhood may be formed, and how it develops and changes through the life course and beyond. There we will also return to issues of gender and sexuality by examining rituals associated with creating and maintaining cultural constructions of difference; and we will examine more generally the way in which people acquire and express their *identity* within social groups. In chapter 7, we will turn to look at the formation of those groups themselves, and consider ways in which they are defined, for example through language, ethnicity, religion, and shared history. The focus will again be on the *processes* by which boundaries are drawn around them.

The third part of the book will bring the materials we have studied about people in different societies into a global context, both historical and contemporary. Chapter 8 will open by laying out more detailed theories of human origins, in particular ecological/genetic explanations of biological and social differences between human populations, and how they came to settle long ago in widely separated parts of the world. The second part of chapter 8 will examine the resources social and cultural anthropologists use to discuss migration and settlement patterns and the dissemination of cultural forms such as music and food. It will also begin to introduce theories about more recent examples of the process that has become known as *globalization*. The use of this term basically coincides with the extraordinary increase in the speed of the spread of people and ideas in recent decades, and their ability to keep in touch through the facilities of the internet. There are many disciplines that have addressed these issues, and the value of anthropology for understanding the local effects of these global processes through in-depth ethnographic study will be illustrated in several ways in chapter 9.

The final chapter will turn back to the initial subject of how anthropology is practised. It will consider the methods used by anthropologists to gain an understanding of the unity and diversity of peoples that inhabit our now shared worlds and examine how these have been modified to accommodate technological change. It will also suggest ways that students of the subject may put into practice some of the methods they have learned.

1

The human body

In order to consider what it means to be human from an anthropological perspective we start with the most physical manifestation of our humanity, namely our bodies. Whatever our language, social group, skin colour, or facial features, we all share most of the make-up of these bodies, and the way they act and perform. Our sharpest difference is that between ourselves and other animals. First, we will plunge you into the deep end, introducing the genetic research that biological anthropologists have conducted, quite recently, to demonstrate just how similar we all are, despite our physical variety. The evidence points to a unity of human life, illustrating both the declining importance of issues such as race and how we have evolved to differ from other living beings, notably the animals known as primates to whom we are most closely related in genetic terms.

We will then turn to examine the diversity found in the way human bodies are used, and although these differences are not big, in comparison with our shared unity, they offer a wealth of themes for understanding cultural variety. We will look at how our bodies become a canvas for expressing our long-term cultural allegiances, as well as our membership of the fashion-conscious modern world, and we will also begin to think about the variety of ways we use and modify our bodies in different social and cultural circumstances. That will introduce the subject matter that is more of interest to *social* and *cultural anthropologist*s.

The biological body

From the perspective of biological anthropology, the twin influences of genetic transmission and environmental adaptation make up what our human bodies are today, and the technical term used to describe the outcome is *phenotype*. Essentially, this is the result of interactions between our genes and the environment in which we live, and the relationship can be expressed by the formula: *genotype* + environment = phenotype. The exact balance between genes and the environment varies massively from one human *trait* – or characteristic – to another. For instance, height is estimated to be seventy percent genetic and thirty percent environmental; you may have genes that can produce a height of six feet, but if your environment provides insufficient nutrition then your actual 'phenotypic' height will be shorter.

Many of the traits that create a person's observable phenotype, such as skin and hair colour, height and body shape, are well understood; yet some of what we consider to be the 'most human' are not. Intelligence, for example, is perhaps the most human quality, and like all other traits it is the result of the interplay between genes and the environment, but the interplay is not fully understood. Today, we estimate that a person's intelligence is a 50–50 split between their genes and their environment. In this analysis, 'intelligence' is measured by taking a standardized intelligence quotient (IQ) test, but many argue that IQ tests contain biases, such as assuming particular cultural knowledge. They are also said to ignore many aspects of intelligence, such as the ability to absorb and remember ways of living, being able to work harmoniously with others, and being proficient with money while still doing poorly on maths-test questions.

Regardless of the challenges involved in measuring the exact contribution of genes and environment, what is not debated is that humans, like all organisms, are the result of their interplay. In order to understand how human beings have evolved as somehow different from all other members of the living world, we need to examine ourselves within the larger context of that world, and particularly as members of a group of our closest relatives, the apes, monkeys, and chimpanzees whom we also call primates. Our place cannot be really properly understood unless we have an appreciation of exactly how we relate to these other members of the primate order: what we share, both in terms of genes and behaviours, and what makes us all unique. We will examine this aspect of our evolutionary history first, and then return to look in more detail at the environment.

Life as a primate

It was the system of species classification developed in the eighteenth century by the Swedish scientist Carl Linnaeus that defined our human species, technically known as *Homo sapiens*, as belonging to the order of primates. This means, in simple terms, that humans share more similarities with our fellow primates than we do with other organisms. For instance, all primates have broadly similar skeletons, including bulbous skulls or brain cases, fingernails, and mostly generalized dentition rather than teeth for specific purposes.

Primates have another feature which distinguishes us from other organisms in the way that we live in our environments, and that is that we are *generalists*. Rather than being *adapted* to one particular type of diet or habitat, as other living species usually are, we primates are capable of exploiting a wide variety of resources. In essence, primates' key *adaptation*, a technical term used to describe the way living beings live and thrive within a particular environment, is their very adaptability. And what makes humans so different from all the other primates is the huge extent to which we shape and change our environment – not always for the better – in order to suit our needs. Our ability to adapt is unmatched. So while no other primate species has spread throughout the world from its original habitat, humans have populated virtually the whole globe. Our closest primate relatives, the chimpanzees and gorillas, are on the other hand exclusively found (unless in captivity) around the African tropical forests that have been home to their species for millions of years.

Since our primate genes and our lived environment interact, it is helpful to look at how this fork in each primate's evolutionary path has helped to define what we call human, even at the level of the body. In basic terms, the human body is that of a medium-sized African great ape. In keeping with Linnaean classification, the human skeleton shares a large number of traits with the other primates. For example, humans share with chimpanzees similar ways of sensing the world, including sight, hearing, smell, taste, and touch, as well as biochemical processes for activities ranging from the digestion of food to foetal development. Perhaps most startlingly, humans and chimpanzees share somewhere between ninety-six percent and ninety-nine percent of our DNA, the genetic code of life. Still, the differences between humans and chimpanzees appear large, and indeed they are. It is only when we think of humans and chimpanzees compared to a much more distant evolutionary relation, such as a horse, that we see how humans, as a great ape, share so much in common with chimpanzees.

But what of the DNA (like the genetic instruction booklet that controls how all organisms develop and function)? How can one to four percent of difference in the genes of the two species account for such fundamental differences in appearance and behaviour? We must beware the simple answer, for although so much DNA is shared there are also fundamental differences in the organization of those genes. (In fact, humans share forty percent of their DNA with bananas!) This organization is principally about the *order* in which genes (or even genetic bases that make up genes) are strung on chromosomes, which are coiled strands

Table 1.1 Major differences between *Homo sapiens* and chimpanzee biology

	Homo sapiens	*Chimpanzee*
Forehead	Vertical	Low & sloping
Face	Flat	Jutting forward
Cranial vault	Widest at top	Widest at bottom
Brain size	Large	Small
Canine teeth	Small	Large
Base of skull	Angled	Less angled
Lumbar vertebrae	5	3–4
Limbs	Straight	Curved
Limb proportions	Long legs	Short legs
Wrist	Less flexible	More flexible
Hand	Cup-shaped with long thumb	Flat with long fingers & short thumb
Foot	Straight big toe & arched foot	Curved big toe & flat foot
Pelvis	Neonatal head is tight fit	Neonatal head is loose fit
Developmental Period	Slow	Fast

of DNA. While genes may appear on a particular chromosome in humans, they could be on another one in chimpanzees, which affects the way they are expressed as well as the way they combine into multi-gene complexes. Indeed, this is exemplified by the fact that humans have two chromosomes effectively fused into one: hence we have twenty-three pairs of chromosomes and chimpanzees have twenty-four pairs. Another factor is the critical regions of DNA that initiate the activity of other areas of our genetic material, and the presence or absence of these can make a massive difference in the phenotypic potential of a species.

So how has the human ape developed such wide-ranging skills and abilities? It is useful to start by looking at the evolutionary record of the *hominins*, a sub-group of organisms that includes modern humans and all of our related species who are now extinct. Hominin evolution is a story filled with trial and error, told over the span of seven million years. For the first five million years, our ancestors would have looked to our eyes very ape-like, more like an odd-looking chimpanzee. They include a character named *Sahelanthropus tchadensis*, who lived about seven million years ago, and another genus, *Australopithecus*, who lived from about five million years ago until about two million years ago. Yet these species gave rise to later human-like apes, so are considered to be part of the human family tree, or *phylogeny*. The different names of layers you can see in the diagram reflect the relationship between the groups on the family tree – a group of species belongs to a genus, a group of genera belongs to the same sub-family and so on. This structure is used to classify all life on Earth.

Table 1.2 The relationship between extinct and all living primates

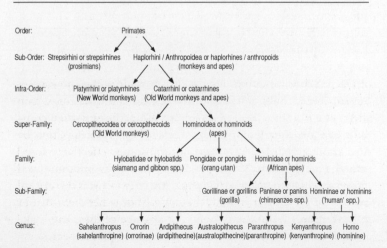

A number of hominin species – between twenty and thirty – followed. Today, there is one: *Homo sapiens,* also known as 'us'. It is not until two million years ago, with the arrival of *Homo ergaster* in the fossil record, that we see hominins that seem to have shared some of the abilities, behaviours, and genes of modern humans. Unlike earlier ape-like hominins, *Homo ergaster* boasted a skeleton very much like our own. This similarity, however, ended above the neck, since their brains were considerably smaller than ours – about 800 cubic centimetres for *Homo ergaster* versus 1250 cubic centimetres for us. Not surprisingly, their skulls were also very different. However, *Homo ergaster* started to exhibit much human-like behaviour, including fire use and complex stone tool making; they probably also used some form of vocal communication, and even perhaps cared for the sick.

Our understanding of human evolution is continually being updated, as new tools become available for studying fossils, the genetic code of DNA, and other sources of information. Originally, anthropologists thought that modern humans were descended from other apes in a single line of species – from *Australopithecus* to *Homo erectus* to Neanderthal to us. In the past fifteen to twenty years, however, amazing new finds and techniques have been used to fill in the picture. Today, anthropologists believe that multiple species existed side by side, though we do not yet know the exact relationships they had to one another. In 2004, one fossil find in Indonesia, the possible species *Homo floresiensis*, forced palaeontologists to question assumptions about what it means to be human – prompting a re-evaluation of human evolutionary development. *Homo floresiensis* demonstrates that although humans can manipulate our environment, we very much remain subject to its whims. It's always important to remember that in biological anthropology we should be cautious of the simple answer, since the story of human evolution is far from simple.

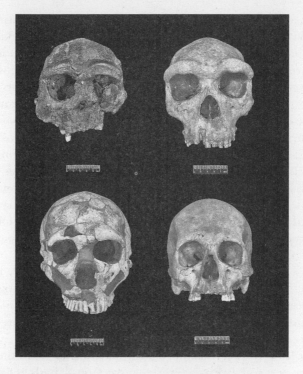

Figure 1.1 Skulls of various *Homo* species. Upper left is *Homo erectus*, around 1.2 millions years old; upper right is *Homo heidelbergensis*, around 300,000 years old; lower left is *Homo neanderthalensis*, around 70,000 years old; and lower right is *Homo sapiens*, or an anatomically modern human.
Natural History Museum, London / Science Photo Library

Evolving environmentally

The impetus for the host of dramatic changes among early humans – such as the use of fire and stone tools – appears to have been a change in the environment. This isn't surprising, since evolution is so dependent on the interplay between environment and genes. One of the most dynamic areas in which we see this interplay in action among humans involves the development of *bipedalism*, or walking on two legs, a trait found only in hominins. If you compare the human body to that of the quadruped chimpanzee (which, as the term suggests, primarily walks on four limbs) and imagine the changes needed to make chimpanzees bipedal, you can see that almost no part of the body would escape change. Chimpanzees are evolved primarily to walk on four limbs (using their knuckles to act as 'feet') and are highly skilled climbers. We can determine the way in which our fossil ancestors moved by examining the way in which their skeletons supported the muscles of the body, which in turn reveal how locomotion occurred – bigger legs than arms suggests walking on two legs while roughly equal-sized limbs suggests using four limbs to move.

It is sometimes said that walking on two legs separates humans from 'the animals' and this idea conforms to the fossil interpretations of biological anthropologists. Bipedalism is the earliest identifiable difference in the fossil record to mark the advent of hominins. Bipedal traits began to appear seven million years ago, with *Sahelanthropus tchadensis*, but these distant ancestors retained a high degree of climbing ability and spent much of their time in the trees. Based on the skeletal remains discovered by anthropologists, the modern form of walking only became possible with the appearance of *Homo ergaster*.

Why did such a drastic and intensive set of adaptations evolve? The answer seems to lie in the environmental conditions existing on the African continent during the Miocene period, a geological epoch that lasted from approximately twenty-four million to five million years ago. Around ten million to eight million years ago, global temperatures dropped, resulting in the fragmentation of the previously large forests of Africa and the development of the savannah, the wide open grassland that characterizes modern East Africa. Biological anthropologists believe this massive change in environment appears to have kick-started human evolution, as our early ancestors ventured out of the now disconnected forests and onto the savannah. The ancestors of chimpanzees stayed in the forest habitat where chimpanzees remain today.

Bipedalism was foremost among human adaptations to the savannah, and one possible reason for the shift to walking on two legs was the scarcity of shade trees: standing means that less surface area is exposed to sunlight, which allowed our ancestors to forage during parts of the day that were too hot for their predators and competitors. Standing upright also left their hands free for other tasks, such as scavenging and butchering meat. These new ways of gathering food in turn provided extra fuel to the ancestral human body, permitting an expansion in human brain size. The brain is an extremely energy-hungry organ, and for ours to have grown so big – 1.5 kilograms on average – required a regular supply of calories. Some time after this expansion in brain size, anthropologists find the first sign of stone tools, around 2.5 million years ago. And these tools allowed early humans to be even more effective at butchering scavenged animal carcasses, and to provide even more energy to supply still bigger brains.

Homo ergaster's skeleton was also extremely well adapted in other ways for life on the open savannah grasslands that dominated East Africa during the Pleistocene period (a geological epoch from 2.5 million to 12,000 years ago). A thick ape fur is of no use in the dry heat of the open savannah, and would have been rapidly lost. As a result, humans developed two further adaptations: the pigmentation of skin to handle the high levels of ultra-violet radiation from the equatorial sun, and the development of sweating as a means of expelling heat from the body. Biologically, the human body is very well adapted to the trials of equatorial heat; that is why humans can proudly claim the title of being the 'best sweating animal'. The body handles cold conditions with less efficiency, which is why we resort to wearing substantial clothes and building extensive shelters in chillier latitudes and altitudes.

Later, we will see in greater detail how our move to bipedalism and the development of bigger brains shaped the human species. In any case, the basic contours of the human body have a deep evolutionary history and should lead us to question many of the assumptions we make about outward differences based on bodies alone.

WHAT IS RACE?

The subject of race spurs as much confusion as controversy. On the surface, we all know that there are different human races, people with different colours of skin and other physical features, don't we? But it's on the surface that the problem lies. The idea of categorizing humans into groups is an old one: who are the members of our family, extended family, village, tribe, religion, region, nation, and a number of other social categories? It's natural to create groups based on perceived differences and we do so based on a huge number of social categories.

But *race* has a specific biological meaning, where it is identical to the term 'sub-species', for groups of organisms within a species that are genetically distinct from one another. So what can we say about the different human 'races'? On the genetic level, there is next to no variation between a person from Africa, Europe, or Asia – pick any two people at random from anywhere on the planet and they will be very closely related when you look at their DNA, much more so than is normal for such a widely dispersed animal species.

The simple fact is that modern biology completely contradicts the way we have traditionally created different human races using skin colour – and European civilization – as the 'standard'. Both ideas are deeply flawed. Skin colour is controlled by a simple genetic switch that controls the production of melanocytes, the cells that produce melanin, which pigments the skin, but this difference is very slight. While the use of European culture as an absolute measure of sophistication simply does not reflect the range and diversity of human society. In short, the idea that there are separate 'human races' simply cannot be sustained in light of twenty-first century biology.

The social body

Because humans share the same basic physical body, it is a prime means for building *social* and *cultural constructions* of widely differing worlds. In this way, the human body is used as a *model* for explaining and understanding the world around us, including the relationships between people. Consider, for example, the way that the names of parts of the body are applied elsewhere in the English language. The *head* stands not only for the feature that tops our physical form, but is also used to describe the person at the top of a school, a family, or a company. The *foot*, on the other hand, can be used to refer to the bottom, say of mountains or of pages. We can extend the 'strong *arm* of the law', much as we would extend its physical equivalent, and the word *heart* is used to speak of central notions such as 'the heart of the matter'. It's also associated with romantic liaisons, of course, when it is depicted in all sorts of cute shapes that don't even look much like the organ that beats inside our chests.

In other languages and societies, parallel uses may be found, as well as stark differences. The word for *head* is used widely to describe aspects of a social or political hierarchy, but with interesting local modifications in its relation to power. In Japanese, for example, the centre of the body is associated with the *hara*, belly or stomach, a word that describes much more than a digestive organ; it is thought that control of the *hara* is essential in maintaining balance or composure. To have the *guts* to carry out a potentially dangerous task attributes another culturally constructed quality to a set of inner organs that again vary in different languages. In several other societies, particularly in the Pacific, the *face* is an important 'front' to present to the world, to conceal or soften inner feelings, and also to protect against insult or shame, as in a 'loss of face'.

These different usages alter the way we perceive the body and the people around us. Other parts of the body may be associated with danger or pollution, and therefore be regarded as *taboo* – prohibited or banned – in some way. For example, for Hindus the right hand is for eating and the left is for cleaning, so to use the left for putting food in your mouth is to break a taboo. As it happens, an early study by the French sociologist Robert Hertz found that the right hand is widely believed to be superior to the left, and in English- and Latin-based languages, the word for *right* is associated with the law (*le droit, el derecho*) as well as with correctness, while *left* is associated with clumsiness (*gauche*) and evil (*sinister*), though these groups do not generally restrict the hand with which a person can eat.

Similarly, in many societies it is regarded as dangerous, and therefore also taboo, for men and women to reveal in public the parts of their body that distinguish them from each other. Yet which parts of the body are deemed taboo to reveal is not at all the same. For instance, a woman in many tropical societies of Latin America and South East Asia may only be required to wear a small apron or cap over her genitals, while in Islamic states, such as Saudi Arabia, a woman in public must wear a flowing robe that covers her whole form, save for her eyes. In nineteenth-century Europe it was regarded as risqué for a woman to reveal her ankles, whereas today in these countries there seems to be little of the legs that needs covering up at all.

These examples introduce the way in which reference to basic differences in the biological makeup of our bodies may be used to express various social systems of *classification*. The socially constructed distinctions between the male and female body, known as *gender* differences, underpin ideas about the abilities of men and women. In some cases, these gender-based abilities are nearly universal, such as the idea that women are defined by their capacity to conceive and feed babies, but there are also many cultural differences. For example, in most agricultural societies, women are thought to be strong enough for taxing physical work; in urban situations, roles that require physical strength were often – until recently – reserved for men. Likewise, the potential for women to hold positions of political or religious power, or those involving or associated with healing skills, varies from one society to another. In fact, in some worldviews, people are divided by age as much as by gender, and in India, Laos, and some Pacific Island communities, certain people may be distinguished as belonging to neither male nor female, but to a third, fourth, or even fifth gender.

The British anthropologist Edmund Leach argued that the English language suppresses words that mark the boundaries of the body, either by forbidding their names in 'polite circles', or by enforcing the use of uncommon Latin terms. He illustrated his point by referring to the products of various bodily orifices as 'exudations', from the Latin word for *ooze*, but take a moment to consider the words commonly used in English for the products of elimination and nose-blowing or for the intimate parts of the body engaged during sex. Even inoffensive-sounding words like *spit* describe a liquid that can be used to express a strong, rude form of disapproval. Terms of abuse also include the names of animals that live in proximity with humans, such as dogs and cats, which he argued is a way of making clear the boundaries between human beings and animals.

Modifying the body

The human body is also a wonderful palette for dressing, decoration, and more permanent modifications such as piercing or tattoos. The variety within one cultural system is matched only by the creative diversity found across the earth. However, those aspects of human decoration that to television directors seem extraordinary enough to present in documentary form, undoubtedly have internal meaning within the cultures where they are found and for anthropologists they provide fascinating areas for investigation.

As we saw above, society imposes on its members expectations about the degree to which the body should be covered, and some basic differences that may be applied to men and women. Clothes and other temporary coverings are also used to distinguish people classified in different ways in any society, and the way people prepare themselves for different occasions. Consider, for example, a school uniform. This dress not only distinguishes humans of a certain age, it marks the particular school the student attends, as well as any differences in social or economic status that this school may imply. Within a school, subtle markers like a badge or a ribbon may express internal divisions like houses, clubs, or teams known only to members of that particular school.

Men who wear business suits are adhering to an almost worldwide directive about the appropriate attire for office wear, though a suit can also convey a great deal about a person, according to its fit or style and its likely cost. In contrast, women in the business world have retained more choice in their clothing, though they must usually conform to rules about how much of their physical body they are allowed to expose. When people dress for a special occasion, very precise rules of apparel may be imposed, for instance, whether a woman must wear a hat to a place of worship. When people have free choice in their clothing, they may be heavily influenced by the fashions of the day, and display expensive brand-name logos, jewellery, or other accessories to indicate a level of economic power, as well as notions of taste. Such distinctions in the selection of temporary coverings are found in all cultural groups, marking a person's position in the group's hierarchy as well as a person's age, occupation, and role at an occasion. In some societies, people wear very little to cover their bodies, but even then the things that they do wear express differences, as illustrated in a renowned study of penis coverings (called sheaths) published in 1969 by Peter Ucko, who detailed the range of coverings found in different locations.

Some of the most flamboyant bodily decorations are displayed at times when an individual is moving from one identity to another, such as when young people enter adulthood. In certain South American tribes, such as the Akwe-Shavante of the Xingu River, people in transitional stages paint their whole bodies, using colours and patterns to indicate family and political affiliations within the tribe. In Japan, there is a day in January when twenty-year-olds mark their entry into adulthood by dressing in kimonos, garments which for many centuries were designed to distinguish status, family allegiance, and between single and married women; the last indicated in the style of the sleeves. People also use their hair to mark such distinctions, and a feature of initiation into adulthood among East African tribes like the Maasai and the Samburu, is to follow a period of allowing youngsters to grow their hair long and unruly with a completely shaven head, painted with ochre to celebrate the attainment of adulthood. Such transitions from one stage of life to another are known as *rites of passage,* and these have often become a central subject area in anthropological studies. (For that reason, rites of passage will be covered in more detail in chapter 6.)

At times, people mark their membership in a group with more permanent modifications to the body. For example, scarification of the face offers a way to demonstrate publicly a person's membership of a clan, while more private modifications such as circumcision may mark acceptance into a religious group, as in Judaism, or the achievement of sexual maturity in the practice found in many societies, but disapproved of in the West, and so described as genital mutilation. In several Pacific societies, tattoos carry meanings, from a person's political position in the Marquesas Islands through commitment to an underworld gang (in Japan) to identity as a 'First', or Indigenous, people for the Māori in New Zealand. An interesting addition to the repertoire of bodily display is found when permanent scarification such as a tattoo is hidden except on special occasions, such as festivals, when Japanese

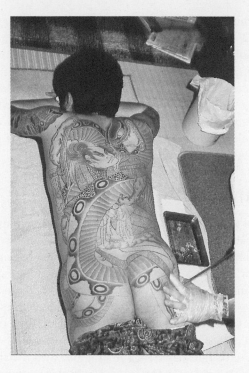

Figure 1.2 A Japanese man having work done on his full-body tattoo.

gangsters may reveal their otherwise hidden tattoos, also used as a way to instil fear in their opponents in times of conflict.

Tattoos and piercings have become common in many urban societies, with a wide range in style and location, but meaning is still embedded in their adoption. There is, of course, the meaning associated with the design itself, but the act of choosing such a bodily modification is also likely to express a fashion, and possibly an assertion of adulthood. Young people thus individualize their bodies as they gradually gain control of them in a society where individual difference is valued. Other examples of bodily modifications include hair colouring, muscle building, and breast implants, all of which allow a person to conform to culturally variable ideas of beauty and attractiveness. In high-tech societies, people may pay to have facelifts to arrest the appearance of the ageing process; it is now even possible to change the biological basis of a person's gender classification, which may have been culturally expressed through cross-dressing, though this kind of practice evokes mixed reactions among different cultural groups.

Using the body

Despite the knowledge that different peoples are brought up to think in other ways about their bodies, it is hard to suppress or hide the shock we experience when we personally come across evidence of different uses, especially in basic matters such as washing, eating, and eliminating waste. These basic reactions are usually triggered on a physiological level by our senses, such as smell and taste, when the familiar feels good, or at least right, and the unfamiliar uncomfortable. Indeed, the emotion of disgust probably exerts the clearest boundary between what diverse people consider to be normal practice in their everyday lives. Notions of dirt and cleanliness are learned so young, and are so intimate, that it is hard to comprehend that other people might have completely alternative views of them, let alone to share or adopt them.

Ways of washing provide a good example. Even where similar technology is available, people may choose to arrange it in quite different ways, and for that reason the bathroom is an advantageous place to examine, as an anthropologist. The relative location of a bath, toilet, and shower is one cultural variable. In some societies, the toilet is kept quite separate from washing areas, as the two are seen to serve distinct purposes; in others, a source of running water is placed right beside the toilet because it is considered unhygienic to use paper to clean yourself after elimination. A popular Japanese toilet has a small jet for washing right inside the bowl! In China, the shower is sometimes located immediately above the toilet, as the same pipe can carry away the used water from both conveniences, but standing on the footprints of a hole-in-the-floor toilet may seem an unclean way to wash for others.

The degree to which the bathroom is a private place is another interesting marker. Within one family, people may wander in and out of the bathroom freely, but lock the door for visitors; in another, each member of the family may prefer their own private space; in yet another case, the bathroom may be open for visitors to use as and when they need it and shutting the door may seem an unfriendly act. This last example may be perceived as overly personal, an idea which could be mirrored in public toilets, which have varying degrees of privacy built in to their overall construction: some have a row of open stalls; others are firmly enclosed in compartments. There are also plenty of places around the world where the open countryside is used for these practices, and it may be a cheerful daily routine to go out with friends or family members to attend to bodily hygiene.

Ways of eating provide another lens for observing different uses of the body, alongside the variety of things that are regarded as edible at all. Because humans are so adaptable, we have been able to select quite distinct diets from the foodstuffs available locally and eat them at different times and in different ways. Peoples have also found a variety of ways of gathering, cultivating, preparing, and refining their daily sustenance. Some regard as delicious plants – like seaweed – that others leave for different species. Likewise, some eat animals that others regard as sacred or polluting that have therefore become taboo for the table, such as the sacred cows of Hinduism or the polluting pigs of Islam and Judaism. In fact, using a table at all is itself a culturally variable feature! A characteristic of the multicultural, urban societies in which many people now live, is that so many foodstuffs are available that our bodies rebel, and grow sick or obese, notably from snacks and fizzy drinks that have replaced natural sustenance like nuts, berries, milk, or coconut milk. An interesting turn of fate is the way that those with most choice of cheap, refined food are turning to their gardens or allotments to grow fresh food, while others choose 'organic' foods free from the chemicals that were developed to protect them.

All these aspects of the use, abuse, and embellishment of the human body come with social and cultural meanings, and in subsequent chapters of this book, we will seek to explain and interpret features we have raised here within the wider contexts of the activities of specific social groups.

2
Ways of thinking and communicating

Having considered in some detail the bodies we human beings share, we move to look at two characteristics that humans often consider part and parcel of our humanity: namely, our ability to think and our ability to communicate our thoughts with others.

This time we will start with the analysis of social anthropologists who work with their contemporaries, because an important part of our work is precisely to understand the ways that people think and communicate, especially those who have been brought up differently from ourselves. Learning language is vital to this endeavour, and later in the chapter we will look at ideas about how humans developed their use of speech, but first let us demonstrate how broad the notion of language can be.

In order to express our thoughts, we need some kind of language, and almost as soon as we enter the world as babies, we begin to learn such a thing. At first, it is very basic. Crying demonstrates that we are alive, and need sustenance, but pretty soon afterwards communication includes interaction with, and reflection of, the language of members of our social group, probably starting with smiles and other facial expressions. This chapter starts with the concept of *socialization*, which is the process by which human babies learn to be part of the societies into which they are born, and how to *classify* the world they encounter. In the previous chapter we talked of Linnaean ideas of classification of animal species; here we turn to the way that humans classify the world around them, an activity that organizes the way we think, and which varies considerably from one social and linguistic group to another.

Ideas about thinking lead to ideas about *rationality*, and just as the systems of classification vary, so do the ways in which people *rationalize* what they do and say. So actions that seem irrational to one group may be seen to be perfectly rational within the system of classification of another. There are many possible ways that this can be explained and demonstrated, but we have chosen an example that we think is particularly powerful, namely, different ways of explaining misfortune, and this will form the subject matter of the second section of the chapter. This will take us into the realm of what anthropologists call *ways of thinking*.

Later, we will turn to consider what we may call *ways of communicating*, which of course include spoken language, but also the use of all kinds of symbolism. In the last section we will look at the work of biological anthropology on all these subjects, notably the evidence for the earliest languages.

Socialization and classification

Because ways of thinking and communicating in any society are learned when we are very young, they seem natural and normal, like our use of the bathroom. As adults care for, speak to, and play with their babies, they are at the same time gradually turning a biological being into a social being, who will learn as it grows to share the language he or she absorbs, spoken and unspoken. Babies pick up signals through all their senses, and the emphasis on communicating through different senses is another variable feature from one social group to another. Sounds, for example, which babies may at first seem to use indiscriminately, gradually take on a meaning shared with the surrounding adults, and they soon learn when and where it is appropriate and useful to apply those sounds to maximum effect. They also learn when some other form of communication, such as smiling, laughing, or crying, might transmit better what they have in their highly absorbent minds.

During this process, babies are all the time learning to *classify*: to form the shapes, sounds, smells, and tastes around them into recognizable things which can be named, distinguished from each other, and added to a specific *category* among those available in their own language and social group. The closest living beings will likely become *Mum* and *Dad, Nana,* or perhaps *Granny, Papa,* and so forth, but eventually, and even more importantly, these will become part of some kind of *family*, which has boundaries between it and the outside world. Later, we will look at different types of family in detail, and how families themselves may form an ordered part of a wider kin group such as a *clan*. Suffice it to say at this point that although all these words may have close parallels in different languages, the social relations the people they mark have to others around them can vary widely.

An early study of classification was made by French scholars Emile Durkheim and his nephew Marcel Mauss who collected information gathered around the turn of the twentieth century by anthropologists from various parts of the world. They discussed the classification of space and time, as well as of people and animals. In his introduction to the English translation of their now classic book *Primitive Classification*, the Oxford anthropologist Rodney Needham points out that an anthropologist learning a strange system of classification may be compared to a blind person who is suddenly given sight. At first, everything seems a blur, with no clear shape or meaning, and only gradually can he or she replace their own firmly ingrained system of thinking with a new one that classifies things quite differently.

For example, from the same world that sees the sun rise and set daily, that sees the moon wax and wane monthly, and that watches a variety of seasons come and go on an annual basis, there are many way of classifying this timely activity. It is quite common to have a system of directions that includes north, south, east, and west, measured, as elsewhere, in reference to the movement of the sun. Some Native American systems also include the directions of up and down, or zenith and nadir, and even centre, and the example given by Durkheim and Mauss was the Zuni people, using the work gathered by an American anthropologist named Frank Cushing. Their clans were assigned one of the directions, which also have animals and plants associated with them, as well as aspects of colour, climate, and character. This helped people to know immediately where to camp when they were travelling, and offered many other ways of making reference to these characteristics.

To aid an understanding of how this kind of classification affects the English language, consider the use of colours in the context of climate and character. Green, which could easily be associated with the fresh growth of spring or summer, is used for people who are ecologically aware, but as a colour for eyes it is also used to refer to jealousy. Yellow, on the other hand, which could be classed as an autumnal colour, is associated with cowardice, as is the chicken! For those who did not know these things, a chicken might be classified as curious, or perhaps noisy. The colours associated with seasons differ in different climates. For example, when the changes are largely between dry and wet, as found in hot equatorial regions, there may be little to compare with the green of a northern spring, whereas in the cold, snowy Arctic, differences might be in how the ever-present snow reflects the light. Indeed, there are anthropological studies of all these possibilities, for the classification of colour and sheen vary too. Not to understand such systems of classification could be to miss all kinds of subtle forms of communication within any one language.

Another area discussed in some detail by Durkheim and Mauss was the classification of time. They noted the twelve Chinese signs, which mark each year as associated with a particular animal or bird. They also pointed out that each day, and even each hour, can be further classified as associated with one of the five elements: fire, water, wood, metal, and earth, each in an aspect of yin and yang. Such associations have fascinating implications, thought to affect the character of a child born on a particular day, or to make a day good for doing business, or carrying out a wedding or a funeral. Such a system affects decision-making in Chinese communities around the world, and it is different from, though comparable to, the Western astrological signs, which may have some of the same implications.

The language of classification orders the way we think in any language. This need for human beings to classify what they encounter was explained by the influential French anthropologist Claude Lévi-Strauss, who considered it to be a universal feature of the human mind. Lévi-Strauss collected a large number of legends and stories to demonstrate a common underlying structure to the various systems of classification. The American linguist Edward Sapir, and his student Benjamin Whorf, hypothesized that we can *only* think through language, and our language thus constrains our very perceptions of the world. To think in another language involves adopting a different system of classification, which we would again absorb early if we grow up multi-lingual. Otherwise, it is useful for students of anthropology to take on board Rodney Needham's idea about the blind being given sight. It may take quite a while to realize just how different languages can be, and how easy it is for people to misunderstand one another.

Explanations of misfortune

An important method that anthropologists use to learn about ways of thinking is to consider how people explain and deal with misfortunes that happen to them. On such occasions, people draw on ideas that they have been socialized to share but which may or may not be apparent in everyday conversation as they may be taken for granted. These ideas are often related to religion, a spirit world, or a system of classification that draws on ideas about supernatural powers that some specialist people are believed to control. For others, or even for the same people in different situations, answers are found in *science*, and again most people would turn to specialists – doctors or engineers perhaps – for help in solving particular problems. In all cases, they are drawing on a *cosmology*, a system of ideas about the world, how it is classified, how it works, and how they fit into that world.

An influential study on this subject was published in a book named *Witchcraft, Oracles and Magic among the Azande* by E. E. Evans-Pritchard, whose fieldwork in the Southern Sudan enabled him to discover and explain a rather different system of logic to the one he started out with. The Azande people draw on ideas of witchcraft to explain unfortunate things that happen in their lives. For them, witchcraft is not something frightening, as it might be for people in Britain, but simply an annoying everyday occurrence. It was, therefore, brought frequently to the attention of the anthropologist learning their language, and Evans-Pritchard explained that the logic behind this use of the term provides a complete explanation for unfortunate events, such as crop failure, accidental injury, or illness.

This doesn't mean that the Azande are unaware of 'natural' explanations. If a person falls over a root in the path, they know that the root caused them to trip; if their crops fail because of a lack of rain, they know that they needed water to thrive; if members of a family fall sick after eating something unusual, they know that it may have been bad. What witchcraft explains in all these cases is why that bad thing happened to those particular people at that particular time: why the person who tripped walked that way, why the rain fell elsewhere and missed the crops, and why the ones who fell sick happened to eat that food on that day. To explain such things in terms of having been bewitched takes an explanation that others may simply wonder about to a complete logical conclusion, he argued.

The advantage for the Azande is that they know how to react to being bewitched. They have various methods of divination to which they can turn, and Evans-Pritchard saw this as an important aspect of their ideas. If we are hurt, and we can find a way to alleviate that hurt, we all feel a bit better about it, even while the hurt is still healing. For many of us, this would entail going to a doctor, or another kind of healer; others might resort to prayer, or visit a shrine to ask for healing from a divine power. Azande diviners will try to find out who was responsible for the bewitching, and then advise the victim on the procedure necessary for approaching the person to ask them to desist.

Especially intriguing here is that the perpetrator may not be aware of having bewitched someone, despite being thought to possess the innate power to do it. According to Azande thought, the power is activated only if there is some further tension between the parties involved. Thus, when considering who might have brought about such an affliction, one considers whom one might have offended. To approach the person divined as responsible is to bring the tensions out into the open, argued Evans-Pritchard, and thus to offer a way of resolving bad feeling. A final piece of his argument is that, knowing this, Azande try hard not to offend each other, so this whole *way of thinking* encourages good interpersonal relations. This was quite a lot for the anthropologist to gather from one everyday word ... unusual for him, but crucial in the lives of the Azande.

In other situations, a similar way of dealing with misfortune may be found by quite different means. For example, it is not uncommon for people to think that they are suffering in some way because they have offended God, or some other spiritual power, and they may pray, or consult a priest or other leader, to see how they can adjust their behaviour for the better.

Others may think they have upset a relative who has died, in which case they might turn to a medium who can enable communication with their dead relative and ask what they must do differently in order to appease that relative. In other words, they look to their own behaviour to see if they are somehow causing the misfortune themselves; seeking help from a doctor or a nutritionist could be interpreted in the same way. All these reactions rely on a system of rationality that reflects what anthropologists call a cosmology – ideas about how the world works.

SCIENCE EXPLAINS MISFORTUNE

Even when people seek help from *science* for an ailment, they are usually putting themselves in the hands of a *specialist* who calls on a *belief system* that the patient may not personally fully understand. The doctor, too, brings into play mechanisms for healing that may have been tried and tested, but there is also an element of *faith* that the medicine, or surgery, will do what is expected, according to the state of the science at the time. Sometimes this simply does not happen, and the medical profession talks of future research. Looking beyond the system of medicine that is accepted by hospitals around the world – sometimes referred to as the cosmopolitan system – there are many 'folk' or 'indigenous' practices which may be just as effective in relieving pain or other suffering, perhaps more so, but which have no explanation in orthodox terms. Should they be ignored? An anthropologist would seek an internal logic for the system in question, and it is likely that this would be available, especially if the local language is understood. Chinese medicine is a good example, for its own system of logic is based around a notion called *qi*, sometimes translated as an 'energy flow', with which a practitioner interacts, but many peoples around the world have their own ways of dealing with sickness and other misfortune, and it would be a mistake to dismiss them as irrelevant because they are not understood in 'scientific' terms.

Forms of communication

An anthropologist can only gain this depth of understanding in a society by learning the language its people use to communicate amongst themselves, and we need to take into account internal subtleties of the language, including non-verbal hints such as facial expressions and tone of voice. Levels of politeness must be considered as well as local dialectical variations, and it is also possible for members of a society to communicate at different levels with different people around them. Age-mates usually share a language that differs from that used in communication between age groups – parents and their teenage children would be one good example, and words like 'cheers' and 'wicked' have taken on completely different meanings in recent UK speech. Men and women may also use quite different ways of speaking, especially when they are in a single-sex situation. Specialists in particular fields also develop a vocabulary for their own area of expertise, and ordinary members of all kinds of interest groups share a certain level of internal jargon.

There are also certain words in a language which are avoided in some kinds of company indeed there may well be whole subjects which are virtually *taboo*. A noteworthy study carried out by anthropologist Allison James in a Yorkshire village found that it was not really acceptable to talk about mental illness, and a man who continued to plough again and again a field which he had already completely turned over, was simply accepted as eccentric. More worryingly, there are studies that demonstrate the uselessness of overseas aid aimed at eradicating dangerous diseases such as HIV/AIDS because those who have been employed to introduce the issues fail to take on board the impossibility of raising intimate details of health directly. Helen Lambert carried out a study with women and aid workers in India which illustrates very clearly the importance of understanding and being able to use euphemism and other forms of indirect communication.

On a lighter level, humour is a very variable feature between languages, and it is often difficult to translate jokes, even between related European tongues like French, German, and English. Indeed, each language has a fund of jokes about the others, well illustrated in a television programme, *Allo Allo*, about French resistance during World War II. Among several African peoples, teasing and joking may be acceptable between some persons but not others, and the joking relationships of the Mende cousins in Mali are rather well known. Relations between a man and his mother-in-law provide another example, described by British anthropologist Alfred Radcliffe-Brown back in 1940, and these contrast with the situation among some Aboriginal peoples in Australia, who must avoid their mothers-in-law altogether. An anthropologist working in any of these societies must build up an understanding of the local customs in order to communicate properly at all, and there is nowadays a fine dividing line between joking and being politically incorrect.

It may also be a matter of self-defence to build up an ability to behave in a manner appropriate to any occasion a visitor from outside might encounter. James Howe and Joel Sherzer went together to work on an island in the Caribbean. Known locally as Friend Hairyfish and Friend Rattlesnake, they had many problems as they tried to work out local versions of humour and deception. In an article recounting some of their excruciating experiences they give examples of the way the people with whom they were working would purposely lie to them – even on one occasion reporting the death of each to the other. They eventually conclude that this local way of communicating also served the important purpose of keeping them in their place in this society, and indeed, this is an important principle enacted everywhere in different ways, perhaps explaining the widespread use of care in communication between in-laws.

Telling lies is not uncommon actually, and the practice may serve a variety of communicative purposes. In some cases, lies are disapproved of in principle, but they might be used to avoid hurting someone, or justified to keep oneself out of trouble. In other cases, lies are used for political reasons, and the acceptance or otherwise of such practice differs widely from one society to another. In many Pacific Islands, it is entirely inappropriate to speak directly about an issue of dispute, and ways must be found to resolves differences of opinion without referring directly to the matter in hand. In *Dangerous Words,* edited by Donald Brenneis and Fred Myers, the issue is explored in many examples, and it seems to come close to what in English we call *diplomacy*. Elsewhere, for example in Greece and many Middle Eastern societies, there is a strong idea that knowledge is power, and talking too freely is discouraged, a practice that may well be misinterpreted by outsiders who might see it as a 'cover-up' or a sign of corruption.

To get an idea of how these forms of communication vary from one language to another, it may help to consider different uses of English found in different English-speaking communities. The politeness of American strangers may seem unduly loud and gushing from a British perspective, while the British might seem cold and distant to outsiders in a parallel situation, hence their description as phlegmatic, or 'dour' in the case of the Scots. There are also notable differences between the north of England, where it is not only acceptable but sometimes expected to chat with strangers, and the south where this is usually avoided. In Canada and Australia, there is a wonderful ability to make light of unexpected difficulties, and British visitors may find they get nowhere by complaining – indeed in Australia we have earned a reputation as 'whinging poms' for such behaviour. Even within any one of those nations, there are regional variations in humour, and the degree to which it is acceptable to speak directly.

There is also a whole range of communication that goes beyond the spoken word, and in many languages, non-verbal cues are vital in making sense of the words spoken in any situation. Facial expressions provide one example, gestures another, and care needs to be taken not to misinterpret something that looks familiar, so an innocent use of the fingers in one context can be a serious insult in another. The thumbs–up sign is one example – a positive indication of agreement or approval in the UK and other Western countries, but disgusting and possibly insulting in parts of the Middle East. There are also places such as Japan, China, and Thailand, in which a smile is a kind of cover up for sadness or shock, and it would be a gross misunderstanding to interpret it as a sign of pleasure, or a shared expression of friendship, for example.

On the other hand, there are examples of communication that can link or separate people, regardless of their background or their mother tongue. The language of soccer is one global example, usually involving the names of current stars and their recent activities; others are related to computer games, or the latest Japanese or Korean cartoon characters and the stories of their animated films. Virtual communication is a chief characteristic of the world of the internet, and the various networks such as Facebook and Twitter are sometimes seen as having taken over in importance from personal contacts. Such facilities allow people who might never meet, but who share interests or particular concerns, to communicate and to support each other. An interesting study, entitled *Natives on the Net,* analyses the contribution of cyberspace to the resurgence of power amongst Indigenous peoples whose voices have been suppressed for several generations.

Not all languages have a written script, and a form of communication that has been threatened by the rise of new technologies is the art of storytelling. In pre–literate societies, some people could remember and recite laws, legends, and stories that would last for hours, and when the invention of the written word made such feats unnecessary, humans began to lose the ability. Consider ways in which we have replaced the experience of listening to stories … perhaps by listening to the radio, reading blogs or tweets, watching films or television, or by going to the theatre. The importance of narrative style has not been lost, however; perhaps it has just been expanded and developed into different media, and our human powers of communication are being stretched yet again.

Symbolic communication

All these kinds of communication form what anthropologists call symbolic communication. Symbolism forms a kind of language, just as language is a kind of symbolism, where words or phrases stand for the things they represent. The sounds that stand for particular things in any one language are otherwise completely arbitrary, as can be evidenced by the different sounds that stand for the same thing, or something very similar, in a different language. More commonly recognized as symbols are the objects we use to communicate things like wealth and status – top brand trainers, smart mobile phones, and the latest fashion in clothes and accessories.

What then do we mean by a *symbol*? Dictionaries offer several definitions, but a concise amalgamated one could simply be 'a thing regarded by general consent as representing or standing for something else'. This definition would also work for a sign, but in general a sign can be explained very easily – at the traffic lights, red stands for stop, green stands for go – whereas interpreting a symbol is usually more complicated, and the symbol itself is a powerful means of communication that cannot simply be replaced by a few words. Symbols form very good data for anthropologists to collect and study, then, for their complete understanding is usually limited to one language or social group, and to gain access to their use is to gain an understanding of the ways of thinking of that group.

Earlier we considered the way that dress, hair, and more permanent bodily modifications may communicate membership of an age group, an occupation, or a position of power, and these are all examples of the use of bodily symbolism. In complex urban societies, where people from different backgrounds mingle in public places, some of them choose to express their social or religious origins in symbols they wear. Examples include a turban for a male Sikh, a head scarf and face veil for a female Muslim, and the little knitted cap known as a *kippa sruga* for a Jewish male. In Mexico and Guatemala, members of particular indigenous groups travel to the town and city markets in dresses or blouses that mark – or symbolize – their membership of the society from which they hail. Such distinctions are also demonstrated by the use of flags and other regalia, where a cross usually stands for Christianity, a crescent moon for Islam, and the shape of a dove for peace.

Animals offer another *marker*, or symbol, and those that in one society may become pets or food, may in another take on a special role associated with clan membership. These animals were called *totems* by some anthropologists, for the way they may manifest spiritual or sacred qualities, especially for members of that particular clan, understood properly only within the system of classification shared in that society. It may also be that they are forbidden from eating, or that only members of the associated clan are allowed to eat them. Either way, they are *marked* out as special for that group. This term, *totem*, has also been used to describe the big, carved poles built by some of the Native Peoples of Canada (who call themselves First Peoples). Here the clans do adopt animal names, but the poles might be built to mark a special occasion, or the establishment of a new venture, and are not necessarily associated with clan membership, so care needs to be taken to understand this term in its local context.

These distinctions demonstrate again the subtlety of communication within a particular language and society, which

Figure 2.1 Totem poles in Vancouver's Capilano Park illustrate a number of First Nations stories; this shows one about a raven who rescued the sun when it was stolen by a selfish chief.
Photograph by Joy Hendry

illustrate the difficulty for an anthropologist of getting a really deep understanding of the possibilities. In the complex multicultural world many people now inhabit, the ability even to see this depth is a valuable skill, vital to easing communication between people of differing backgrounds, and the better we come to understand each other, the smoother our communication should become. We will return again and again to language and symbolism in the chapters that follow, but first let us turn to consider the rather tricky question of how human beings developed language and other communication skills at all.

Languages of the past

It is not really hard to understand the reason why language has evolved – it simply improved communication. Once you move from basic individual subsistence (seen for instance in the behaviour of a rat) to more complicated forms of group-based activity, practised by many of the higher primates, then the need for an effective means of communicating becomes a pressing selective pressure in evolutionary terms. A basic model of language evolution sees gestures and different vocalizations being used to convey basic meaning, gradually developing into a more complex system that allowed intent to be signalled. This proto-language was then thought to gather complexity, mirroring the pattern of increasing brain size seen in the hominin fossil record.

This is not the only view, however. The anthropologist Robin Dunbar suggests instead that social complexity would have been the key driver that led to the evolutionary need for complex language skills. Through the study of non-human primates, who groom each other to maintain social links, Dunbar hypothesized that language evolved in humans as a means of maintaining such links when groups became too large for regular grooming. Language would also have provided a very useful tool for managing intra-group relationships. Speaking not only allows for positive interactions but also less honest behaviours such as lying. This line of thinking would suggest that language has a very close relationship with the evolution of intelligence and social complexity.

Language is unquestionably the great evolutionary gift that really sets us apart from other animals, but its presence in the past

Figure 2.2 Aboriginal rock paintings in Australia record stories that have been handed down for thousands of years; this painting, found in Kakadu National Park, shows people dancing.
Photograph by Joy Hendry

is extremely difficult to detect until the first writing appears on clay tablets a mere six thousand years ago. Clearly, complex unwritten language must have been present before this point so the questions focus on when it appeared and which species of hominin first possessed the ability.

There are a number of sources of evidence available to us to try to answer these questions. First, examining the rough external shape of the brain gives us a sense of how well developed the areas are that are associated with communication in earlier hominins. This investigation is achieved by the moulding of *endocasts* (quite simply, a cast of the inside of the skull), but these models can only provide very rough information which, as our understanding of brain functions develops, is only of limited use. A cautionary tale can be seen in the work of the nineteenth-century French anatomist Paul Broca who thought that intelligence had a direct correlation with brain size. A part of the brain known as Broca's area is associated with controlling the mechanism of speech and is found to be larger in animals with complex vocal communication abilities. In order to test his proposition about intelligence, he measured the cranial capacity (volume in cm3) of a large number of human skulls from different geographical regions and erroneously concluded that Europeans had larger skulls than Africans and Asians so therefore must be more intelligent. Broca was a man of his time and held views on European racial supremacy that are today known to be baseless in biology. Broca had failed to take into account the effects of body size on skull size (and hence brain size) without having any impact on intelligence. Broca left instructions in his will that, after his death, the size of his skull was to be measured. Amusingly, the size of his brain was found to be well below the 'expected' size for a European which he himself had suggested.

Using such endocast evidence, the pattern of development of language we see in the fossil record is not clear – it has been suggested that the two areas of the brain's surface associated with language (Broca's area and Wernicke's area) get bigger from around 2.5 million years ago and can be first seen in a species called *Homo rudolfensis* (2.4 million to 1.8 million years ago). However, other researchers dispute this and argue that it is not until the emergence of *Homo sapiens* two hundred thousand years ago that changes in the size of the language centres of the brain can be detected. Our understanding of the human brain is actually still in its infancy, so we must be cautious about statements linking language ability and/or intelligence based purely on casts of the outside of hominin brains. All we can say with any degree of certainty is that brain size increases over time within the hominin sub-family and that technology and other complex behaviours such as butchery, fire use, and planned hunting appear alongside that development. Once we reach a certain level of cultural ability the question then becomes not did other hominins have language but rather why wouldn't they have had language?

The second set of evidence we can use comes from observing the position of the larynx and pharynx (the voice-producing kit) in skeletal remains. This looks at whether or not the vocal kit was capable of producing and controlling the range of sounds that a complex communication system like ours needs. Within mammals the larynx has two basic positions; high up in the neck in all animals and human infants, allowing breathing and swallowing at the same time, and low in the neck in all adult humans, which means that the airway must be briefly closed during swallowing to prevent food or liquid causing choking (we are all familiar with this as the unpleasant sensation of 'food going down the wrong way'). With the larynx in a low position we are able to generate a very wide range of sounds while all other mammals can only produce a range of sounds by changing the shape of their mouth and lips. In humans the larynx begins to move downward from about two years and reaches the adult position at about age fourteen.

Using this information as a starting point, we can look at the fossil record to determine what sort of vocalization abilities the earlier hominins possessed. For once in human evolution the pattern is very clear. All of the hominins before the appearance of the genus *Homo* around 2.5 million years ago had the usual mammalian larynx pattern (high up, producing a limited range of sounds) while the evidence of a shift to a more human-like larynx position comes with the species *Homo ergaster* two million years ago. This confirms what we saw in the previous chapter, that is, that *Homo ergaster* may be called the 'first human' because of the shape of its skeleton and the complex range of behaviours demonstrated, including use of fire and care for the sick. This leads some people to suggest that *Homo ergaster* had some form of language. The position of the larynx in *Homo ergaster* is similar to that of an eight-year-old *Homo sapiens* child – which suggests the intriguing idea that if this species could 'talk' it would have done so with a rather high pitched voice!

About five hundred thousand years ago a species known as *Homo heidelbergensis* appeared on the scene, and in this case the position of the larynx is broadly identical to ours. When we combine this information with the complex behaviour we see in this species, it seems highly likely that they possessed some form of language. By the time we reach the species known as Neanderthals (250,000 to 28,000 years ago), merely an evolutionary cousin of ours, but with whom we share *Homo heidelbergensis* as a common ancestor, we find that they had the same skeletal architecture for speech that we have and were also so socially developed that it would be impossible to imagine that they did not have complex language.

Finally, we can also use genetic data to address the question of language ability. All mammals possess a gene called *FOXP2* and it has been discovered that mutation of this gene causes severe language problems in humans. It has thus been speculated that the version of this gene that humans have is likely to be a genetic basis for our remarkable language skills. Recent advances in the recovery of 'ancient DNA', which involves recovering DNA from bones, mummies, and other sources, has allowed us partially to reconstruct the genome – the genetic blueprint of an organism – of the Neanderthals. Analysis of the Neanderthal *FOXP2* gene shows that it is exactly the same as the version found in humans. This suggests that both *Homo sapiens* and *Homo neanderthalensis* must have inherited this gene from their common ancestor – namely *Homo heidelbergensis*. This further supports the idea that complex language, while still a purely human ability, was not restricted to *Homo sapiens*, and it also gives us a pretty good idea of when our ancestors developed the ability to communicate in this way.

3
Organizing social relations

Evidence from the excavations of archaeologists and the analysis of their findings by biological anthropologists can offer many hints about the way humans organized relations amongst themselves in the past, and there are numerous studies of our contemporary world by social and cultural anthropologists. In this chapter we will introduce three aspects of the way in which the arrangements of human beings that we have come to call *society* work in a comparative context. First, we will look at the allocation of power, and the extent to which this is passed down through generations, or acquired during a human's lifetime; then we will turn to examine in a little more detail a variety of ways in which the idea of passing through generations may be organized in different parts of the world. Last we will look at some of the material ways in which social relations are initiated and maintained.

Equality, hierarchy, and social power

Human beings in every part of the world organize themselves into groups, and systems of classification provide ways to mark off those groups from others around them, and to organize relations within them. Amongst the members of such a group, there will also be ideas about its organization, which we may call an *ideology*. This may or may not be shared, and the ideas that underpin that organization will influence the way people behave towards one another to different degrees. For example, a notion that we are all born equal is a relatively recent ideology, enshrined in the American constitution but hardly seen in practice in that society. Other nations or social groups in Europe and Asia may have an ideology built on a divine principle of hierarchy, but in practice exercise political power in quite contrasting ways. Actually, all societies can be shown to have a structural form, and individuals within it to exercise a variable amount of control as they grow up in a particular part of that world.

DIFFERENT ANTHROPOLOGIES

Anthropologists have approached the subject of social relations from different points of view. The biological approach, proposed by Herbert Spencer and common in the nineteenth century, was that people formed a 'social organism' that followed the rules of evolution, just like a biological being. The work of scholars such as Emile Durkheim and Marcel Mauss established the discipline of sociology, which focused on the groups formed by human beings that they named societies. Understanding society by looking at systems of classification took its inspiration from the work of linguists, and the aim became one of seeing social relations as a *structure*, with variations in each society, but with a common form determined by the nature of the human brain. Claude Lévi-Strauss was the most famous proponent of this approach, along with anthropologists such as Edmund Leach, Mary Douglas, Rodney Needham, and Alfred Radcliffe-Brown, although each had slightly different ideas of what they meant by 'structure'. The Norwegian Fredrik Barth insisted that we need to start from an individual to understand his or her social relations, and his approach became known as *transactional* anthropology. A major approach initiated by Franz Boas in nineteenth-century America was to start his study from the objects made by human beings in a field and to examine their social relations through this *material culture*. His work laid the foundations of the discipline now called *cultural anthropology*. Today in the United States, those who focus on language in their studies are termed *linguistic anthropologists*.

The structural form may be represented in buildings and monuments, gardens, and other ways that people mark their presence and importance within a social group, and the findings and analysis of archaeologists are full of evidence of what we call *hierarchical* difference. The Egyptians, Aztecs, and Mayan left pyramids, for example, the Romans left roads and baths, and the ancient Polynesians and British left standing stones. Biological anthropologists are able to analyse the relative health of bones found in very different graves, and make links between those containing goods of value with individuals who also demonstrate a superior skeletal health. These findings offer hints, then, about relative *social status*. An example can be seen in Anglo-Saxon burials. High-status males were often interred with swords, shields, and weaponry, designating them as warriors while females were often buried with jewellery and other ornaments such as elaborate hair combs. In addition, there are examples of male Anglo-Saxon skeletons that have been buried with the ornamentation usually found in female burials – the general view is that they were priests and as such seen as being outside of the normal boundaries of gender, but this offers an example of possible complexity.

This is not to suggest that before the dates of these findings our ancestors were incapable of complex social behaviour, but merely that we don't have evidence preserved in the archaeological record. Indeed, in today's world there are plenty of people whose social arrangements exhibit a defined hierarchy, but who have left little for future archaeologists to find. We must be careful not to class them as somehow inferior to groups who do leave a record of themselves. Those societies who left the buildings may have been very brutal.

If we turn to the findings of social anthropologists, we can consider various examples of ways in which status is assigned in society today, and how this status affects relations between us. First, there are qualities that we cannot easily change, which we call *ascribed* status. As soon as a baby is born, or even earlier with modern technology, it is announced to be a boy or a girl. In this way, the child is technically assigned a *gender*, and this will affect relationships with others for the rest of his or her life. In some societies, time is mostly spent with others of the same gender, perhaps even through enforced separation from all but the closest relatives of the other sex. This idea may be reinforced by religious ideology, but even in societies like the US, Europe, and Australia, where gender is supposed to be officially eliminated as a marker of difference, there are usually activities – perhaps doing sports or going shopping – where a strong preference for company of the same gender is still quite evident. There are also ways in which individuals can manipulate the divisions, perhaps by cross-dressing, or these days by surgery, and there are some societies which classify people into more than two genders.

Another aspect of our ascribed status is our age, and quite a range of social life is organized to be carried out in the company of age-mates, though again varying from one society to another. In some East African societies, such as the Maasai and the Nandi, who live in the modern nations of Kenya and Tanzania, society is clearly divided into *age grades*, which play different roles. The older grades take care of political decisions, for example, and try to resolve disputes within the society, whilst the younger adults might be called on to defend the whole group in times of war. As children reach maturity, the grades for boys and girls may organize joint activities at an appropriate time for mate selection, or they may be kept apart until the elders decide the time is ripe to pair them off. All members of society become part of these groups as children, and they move through them together at times considered important for achieving the next status – locally named as approximately equivalent to the English terms youth, young adult, and various levels of senior maturity. People are expected to support one another within a group, and to demonstrate a measure of deference and respect between them.

All societies have ways of classifying people of different ages, and allocate roles according to the local divisions. It is very common for elders to be respected as teachers, though in the society of rapid technological change that many of us now inhabit, older people are sometimes neglected as being out of touch. Instead, youngsters are called to sort out technical problems, but we must be careful not to forget the value of experience. Indigenous peoples across a world that was colonized by great imperial powers value their elders for the cultural knowledge that they hold, and even in the United States and Canada, space is set aside for elders at formal and informal gatherings of Native Peoples.

Another important part of our *ascribed* status comes from the background into which we are born. At a basic level, this is an economic factor: do we have enough to eat to enable our bodies to reach their full genetic potential? Does the society to which we are born have a system of sharing resources amongst its members, or do some sub-groups retain all the wealth and even collect it from others? Ironically, perhaps, groups of human beings who live close to the land, collecting and catching their food, are often much better at sharing it than are those who have found ways to build up wealth beyond their basic needs. American anthropologist Marshall Sahlins described such *hunting and gathering peoples* as the original affluent society, for they all appear to have everything they need. In other cases, a person's prospects may be heavily influenced by the wealth of their parents, or the amount of land they will inherit when they grow up.

Many societies have an inherited system of hierarchy, with chiefs, kings, and queens at one end, and servants or slaves at the other. In India, for example, social relations are organized into stratified groups, or *castes*, with those at the top forbidden to do some dirty tasks for themselves, and those at the bottom called 'untouchables' precisely because they do those tasks. Louis Dumont analyses the Indian system in his classic book *Homo*

Hierarchicus, but again, we should remember that the structural system that underpins this system of classification may be practised in different ways in different parts of the Indian sub-continent, and also in communities around the world that hail from such a system. A book by Declan Quigley entitled *The Interpretation of Caste* examines many examples of the system in practice, and *Contested Hierarchies: a Collaborative Ethnography of Caste among the Newars of the Kathmandu Valley, Nepal,* edited with David Gellner, professor of anthropology at Oxford University, looks at the system in Nepal.

In other societies, social relations may be organized into castes or classes, but roles and expectations might be even more open to manipulation. There is usually at least some measure of status that we can earn by the way we behave, and this is described as *achieved status*. This factor bears a strong relation to the exercise of power within a social group, and it may be more or less overt. Politicians in any society have to work hard to achieve the status they need to exercise power; chiefs, kings, or queens who inherit status still need to act in ways acceptable to their people to maintain their positions, as the bloody testament of history and legend informs us from an early age. There is also a measure of power held in more subtle ways, often by members of society who are physi-cally weaker. Women are said to be 'the power behind the throne'; for example, others of both sexes may build up a reputation for their ability to communicate with the supernatural.

It is always worthwhile to examine some ethnography in detail to see how people gain and exercise power in a particular social system. Luke Freeman has described the situation of a pres-ident of Madagascar from a privileged inside position he gained when working there as an anthropologist as he had previously helped the man who became president with his English language skills. This relationship was beneficial to the president for it gave him access both to a foreign resident with prestigious language skills, and also to some inside anthropological knowledge about his people, in particular how to keep a physical and symbolic distance from them while also demonstrating a connection. The principles of this specific case offer several general elements that can be associated with the acquisition of power in other societies as well.

First, the president had built up a successful business, so he had secured a base of economic power, almost a universal prerequisite for political success. In this case, his business gave him an extra element of prestige, for it had acquired a positive reputation, supplying locally produced goods which he marketed throughout Madagascar. This was but one way in which he managed to arrange a sense of being a part of the people, at the same time as maintaining a physical distance from them through

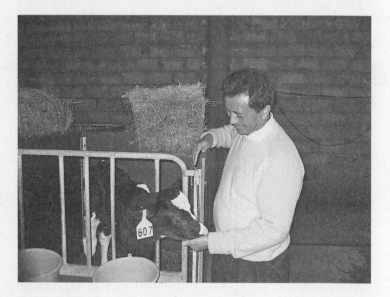

Figure 3.1 President Marc Ravalomanana of Madagascar with one of the dairy cows that made his fortune.
Photograph by Luke Freeman

occupying residential quarters guarded by some considerable military and civil paraphernalia. An occasional appearance became an exciting event, then, which he used to his advantage by choosing moments likely to resonate well with the people.

Freeman describes in some detail the way in which the president built up and maintained this positive image. His business, for example, was based on knowledge of and an ability to operate in a world market, which gave him the prestige of global connections, but he also took trouble to make beneficial donations to local enterprises, and even to send every schoolchild in the country the gift of a satchel. For special events, parades were organized that expressed important elements of the society, again building on the military and civil power that protected his position, but also allowing the participation of many people. An important television broadcast might be made from his office, thus allowing viewers apparently to enter his inner sanctum, a tactic also used to good effect by the US president and the British queen from time to time!

These and further associations mentioned by Freeman are quite specific to Madagascar, but they have their equivalents in many hierarchical systems, especially where the reputation for power needs to be achieved. Success in a venture that is admired locally is a very good starting point, and in the rain forests of South America, hunting skills are important for would-be leaders, who are then able to demonstrate the generosity that is another such quality by giving away much of their cache. In both cases, power lies in an ability to take advantage of opportunities, perhaps also to demonstrate the good fortune that may suggest the co-operation of gods, ancestors or other supernatural beings. A reputation for brutality is sometimes admired, as Freeman again points out, but to offset this with a generosity of spirit may distinguish a big leader from a small-time crook. The ability to change could also be admired, for example, once the fight to gain power is achieved. There are ethnographies that illustrate all these principles and more, and allow the reader to gain an idea of how power must be seen within a social context.

Kinship across cultures

A very important aspect of the social relations we acquire in any society comes from the family, or kin group, into which we are born. This may influence our whole lives, or be something we shake off as we reach adulthood, but it certainly affects the way we start out. In relatively isolated societies, it is quite common to find that everyone is classified as kin in some way, so it is only possible to communicate by knowing one's position within the wider system. Even in quite complex social communities, kin relations may form the basis of the overall political system, as we shall see. In case this seems an alien concept in these days of widespread democracy, consider the history of Europe, and the importance of the aristocratic families that kept us under their control for centuries, though not without drawing on some of the elements of achieving power that we considered in the last section.

The most basic and indisputable unit of kinship is the bio-logical link between a mother and her child, but social aspects of that relationship are created almost as soon as the child is born. Indeed, residence, inheritance possibilities, and group member-ship are often clearly decided even as the child is growing in the womb. In some societies, such as the Ashanti people of Ghana and the Trobriand Islanders of Melanesia, the line created between a mother and her children, is carried through the generations as the most important aspect of social organization, leading anthro-pologists to call the arrangement a *matrilineal* society. Women pass on their name and wealth to their daughters and the principle often extends also to men, who receive property and other kinds of support from their mother's brothers, to whom they might also owe their political loyalties. Birth as a Jew is also inherited through the female line.

In many other societies, these various forms of inheritance are traced through the male line, from father to son, a principle labelled *patrilineal*. It is important, then, that a child be recognized by a father figure, and here the biological link is not necessarily essential. Nowadays, paternity can be established through genetic testing, and this may be the defining feature, but there are many other social mechanisms for giving everyone a place in a patrilineal group. In South America, there are societies where a father will enact some of the behaviour of a pregnant woman alongside her in order to demonstrate his claim to be the father of the child due to arrive, a system known as *couvade*, perhaps a little like a woman taking a birthing partner into hospital in Western countries. Elsewhere, a system we call *polygamy* involves one man taking responsibility for several mothers in order to ensure plenty of progeny in the next generation, and this may also be an accepted way to gain a reputation for power. Problems may arise when people with such practices are subsumed into a nation that forbids it, perhaps because of a Christian rule of monogamy, but polygamy has by no means been eradicated around the world and there are also some societies where one woman may marry more than one man.

Archaeological evidence may give some clues to family relationships, but it is also quite difficult to interpret. One striking example was a burial site found in 1986 at Dolní Věstonice in the Czech Republic, dating to around 26,000 years ago, or the Upper Palaeolithic period. It was a rare triple burial, yielding the remains of three individuals, one female and two males. The female body was in the middle, face up, but partially covered by the two males, who were laid beside her in intriguingly different positions. One was face down while the other was laid on his side and his hands arranged so they reached round the pubic region of the female. The heads of all three were covered with red ochre

Figure 3.2 Skeleton of a *Homo sapiens* human found at the burial site in Dolní Věstonice, Czech Republic.
Pascal Goetgheluck / Science Photo Library

while the female also had red ochre around her pubis. Some researchers have suggested the burial may be that of siblings (because they all have an unusual dental abnormality) while others suggest an adulterous threesome who transgressed a sexual taboo.

Residential arrangements may also make such interpretation difficult because in practice they may not follow the lineal principles, which can gradually be traced as we become more adept at genetic analysis. In a few societies, such as (formerly) the Nayar of Southern India, and even now the Na or Mosuo of Southwest China, sons and daughters continue to live with their mothers throughout their lives, and only liaise with their lovers, including the other parent of their children, on a visiting basis. The suggested taboo in the burial case above could perhaps be interpreted as having arisen in such a situation. Research with people who still practice this kind of living arrangement demon-strates that they do not mean that a child's father is not recog-nized. He may well have a special role to play in the lives of his children, but as one woman may receive more than one man to her home, she needs to choose one to play the role of the father when she gives birth. In the case of the Nayar, there were also strong economic reasons for keeping a group of brothers together to avoid dividing up diminishing plots of land if each were to marry separately.

More commonly, however, some kind of new home is set up between men and women when they marry, though they may live with, or in proximity to the parents of one or the other. If the couple aligns with the family of the wife or mother, we call it a *matrilocal* system; in a *patrilocal* system they join the father's group. In some cases, such as the Nuer and Dinka of the Southern Nile Valley, this last arrangement constitutes a powerful *descent group* of related male kin, which may also form the basis of the political system. Such an arrangement also offers one explanation of the idea that the term for a child's father may also be applied to the other senior male kin. A *matrilocal* system may also have political value, and for several generations in medieval Japan, a family by the name of Fujiwara maintained considerable control over the Imperial Household through marriage: the young princes would be brought up in the homes of their Fujiwara mothers, whose brothers became their consorts as they inherited their roles.

These possibilities for kin relations deepen our under-standing of another aspect of classification: the need for people to distinguish between the relatives on their mother's side (the *mat-rilateral* side) and those on their father's side (the *patrilateral*). In this case, uncles and aunts from each side are clearly distinguished for they may be relatives of quite a different order. In some societies of the Amazonian rainforest, such as the Yąnomamö people, there is even a long-standing rivalry between strong kin groups, and women marrying between them create an important means of alliance, though for them there is the danger of losing contact with their families of birth if such a strategy should fail. Kin relations such as these may influence marriage choices. For example, cousins related through same-sex siblings – fathers and their brothers, or mothers and their sisters – known as *parallel cousins*, may well be forbidden; whereas those related through siblings of the opposite sex, known as *cross-cousins*, may even be encouraged to marry, precisely to form the kind of alliance mentioned above.

The offspring of such a union may ensure the continuity of land tenure, animal husbandry, or even a manufacturing business. To understand a system of kinship properly, it is important to look at the economic and political arrangements of which it is part, and the ethnography of particular peoples will explain the extent to which kin relations, real or fictive, form the basis of wider relations. An excellent study of the families of big Japanese industrialists that have become successful all over the world, for instance, demonstrates very clearly the value of clever marital alliances, and the important role women may play in a society which still usually presents men as the public face. The anthropologist Matthews Masayuki Hamabata in fact set out to study the world of these men, but his limited Japanese, as a second generation Japanese American, put him in an inferior position with the men, which meant he was often in the company of women. However, he discovered in this way the vital role that they played through marriage which had until then been much less well understood! Such serendipity is not unusual in anthropological fieldwork, and we don't always know what we are looking for when we set out to understand another people.

In any society, it is important to look at the kin relations within their wider context of political and economic relations, and to check how the various principles we have outlined work together. We cannot assume that women have more power in a society which emphasizes the *matriline*, although we can look locally for the effect of that principle; neither must we assume that because we see men in the public eye, they are the only ones who wield power. This is one of the reasons why an anthropologist who spends a long time with one people is able to make a study that goes into more depth than any that focus on only one aspect of that society, where some of the inside factors may be overlooked. The overall comparative view is also valuable, but the internal view may be harder to get access to.

Commodities and exchange

A crucial factor to consider in understanding social relations in any society is the use of objects, such as gifts and commodities, to express and negotiate those relations. In relatively isolated communities, which were often chosen by anthropologists for study in the early days, a good map could be made of relations within that community simply by observing the paths being followed as material things were carried to and fro. A hunter might bring meat back to his family, but any that could not soon be consumed within the close group would be distributed more widely, and, as mentioned earlier, a good hunter aspiring to leadership could build up support in this way. In such a society, raw meat from the hunt would be distributed among fellow hunters, while cooked meat is more likely to be shared within the immediate family, and again, people who prepare the cooked meat will have control over how it is distributed and the relations that distribution expresses. In all societies we share food with people we know, and the people with whom we eat are usually related to us in some way.

In other societies, living animals and their produce are used to make and consolidate social and economic relations. For example, for groups of people who make a living by herding, known as *pastoralist societies*, animals are their prime wealth and they may use the products of their animals to secure grazing rights.

An ethnographic study by John Campbell describes the situation of the Sarakatsani shepherds in Greece, who travel quite extensively in the hills, but always take care to present cheese and other produce to the land-owners who permit the grazing. Campbell calls this a *patron-client* relationship. Many African peoples herd cattle as the basis of their economic life, and here the animals are used, for example, to validate a marriage, usually setting up a series of exchanges between groups living some distance apart so that cattle need to be transferred between them. In the early 1950s, Monica Wilson wrote of such practice among the Nyakyusa people of Malawi and Tanzania, pointing out that 'cattle are continually driven down the paths of human relationships'. The anthropologist John Beattie went further to say that the paths that cattle make in these societies actually mark out relations between the humans who herd them.

In a similar way, the movement of material goods expresses relationships between people, and these may help to build up a picture of the symbolic system that operates in their society. Consider a study by Bronisław Malinowski about the people of the Trobriand Islands, off the coast of Papua New Guinea, whom he called the 'Argonauts of the Western Pacific', in reference to the brave sailors of Greek mythology. The system there involved the circulation of armbands and necklaces made of local shells amongst the peoples of a group of quite widely scattered islands. Beautiful boats are built to carry the shells, and the armbands travel in one direction around the islands, the necklaces the other. These are handed over in a ceremonial fashion, and the custom is that they stay only for a limited period in one place, before they must be passed on. In this way, the people maintain contact through these exchanges, and other more mundane exchanges of food and daily goods follow in their wake.

Trobriand men gain prestige through these exchanges, and another study carried out by a female anthropologist called Annette Weiner revealed a parallel system of exchange carried out by the Trobriand women that gives them a different kind of status and power. They make and give away mats and cloths, and in this case custom dictates that the giver retains a hold over the receiver of the goods. In both cases, the gifts are made strategically to ensure the continuity of relations that are considered important to the people, first between different islands, and second between family members linked for co-operation, marriage, and other family matters.

In fact, gifts are very often made strategically, although this may sound a little alien to those who associate them largely with birthdays and Christmas. Consider, for example, the 'free gifts' we are offered when we are out shopping, or that drop through the letter box unexpectedly. In the first case, the offering will probably be an encouragement to taste or try out a commodity that the donor hopes you will like enough to come on in and buy; in the second, it may perhaps be a free pen that the donor hopes you will use to write a cheque to their charity. Visitors to Japan often find they are inundated with gifts from their local acquaintances, and it is important to understand the symbolic language at play here. First, a small gift is a way of opening relations, so it is a friendly wish to make contact; later, other gifts may move to and fro simply in the normal course of neighbourly life – should the gifts become large and expensive, however, they may be followed by the asking of a favour!

A system of exchange that has been much studied by anthropologists and others, known as *potlatch*, is found amongst First Nations of Canada and the Pacific Northwest of the United States. It is a kind of grand giveaway, which often accompanies a special occasion, such as when totem poles might be built. It needs to be seen in a long-term context, for one group might give away so much on one such occasion that they seem to be pauperizing themselves; in the long-run they will receive goods from others, however, and the whole system was interpreted by the American anthropologist Franz Boas, one of the founders of cultural anthropology, as a vital part of their socio-economic system. The crucial factor here is that the more one could give away the more prestige one would gain, and future social relations, including trading partners and even marriage agreements, might depend on this prestige, so it was an important investment. The Canadian government misunderstood the meaning of these events and banned them for a period, but happily they are legal again now, and still take place.

A similar conversion of wealth into prestige may be found in the Mexican system of funding the abundant fiestas that take place in local communities. Those who can raise the resources offer to sponsor a fiesta, pay for the food, decorations, and fireworks and thereby gain the prestigious position of *mayordomo* for that year. This system has also been interpreted as a kind of defence mechanism for those who gain wealth in a society where there is a strong feeling that there is a limit to the goods available to share, and if one family becomes excessively rich, it would be dangerous not to make such donations. On the other hand, some families put themselves into debt to join the group that also gets to make political decisions, a by-product of the acquisition of wealth. The theory of 'limited good' that underpins this system has become rather familiar in these times of worry about using up the planet's resources.

More than one hundred years ago, the French anthropologist Marcel Mauss brought all these ideas about exchange together in a highly influential little book translated into English as *The Gift*, though its French title *Le Don* has a broader meaning that has been translated into English as 'prestation', which basically means something exchanged. One of his most powerful arguments is that for small-scale societies that have no monetary economy all kinds of social, economic, and moral relations, for social groups as well as individuals, may be described in terms of such prestations, which might include entertainment and hospitality as well as material goods. Mauss argued that these exchanges may in theory be voluntary, but in practice, if relations are to work in any particular social context, there are three obligations, namely to give, to receive, and to repay.

In other words social life in its various forms is based on exchange, and many have argued that the principles he outlines are by no means confined to societies that have no complex economy. Some aspects of the latter draw on the same principles mentioned above, the difference being that an individual may refuse a so-called free gift if they have no interest in the relationship, whereas in a relatively isolated society, there is less choice. Once a gift is accepted, however, a relationship is opened, as new contacts demonstrate in Japan, and if one accepts that exchanges also include meals, conversation, and even gossip, they certainly form the basis of most social life! A nice study by Gerd Baumann of Christmas gift exchange between people from various religious backgrounds in Southall, England, demonstrates that the original Christian meaning of a gift can also be quite transformed as the nature of social relations is broadened to make new non-Christian neighbours into members of a wider social group.

4
Engaging with nature

Humans live and interact in a broad context, which we call our environment. Over time, the human body has adapted to the environment in which it has evolved, and as factors such as temperature and altitude have varied. Humans have also developed diverse *cultural* ways to classify this *natural* world, depending on how they make a living out of it. Contrasting perceptions of "nature" sometimes come into quite severe conflict, as we shall see. However, people have also creatively used their environment to make what we call *material culture*, objects which open doors to understanding a variety of artistic and spiritual worlds that have been constructed beyond nature.

Adapting to the environment

Examining the human body tells us the story of how we have adapted to the environment during our history as a species. Although there appears to be an enormous amount of variation in humans – for instance, we all look different, and different parts of the world have different 'types' of humans – this is only partially true. The range of variation we see across the human species is actually the result of two aspects of our historical interaction with the environment. According to evolutionary theory, these may be divided into *natural selection* where an organism adapts to its surroundings for survival, and thus humans adapt in different ways depending on the climate and other conditions; and *sexual selection*, where humans have adapted to the needs of obtaining a mate.

One of the most frequently asked questions about humans, and one that helps us to understand our relationship to the environment is: are we still evolving? This is a question that provokes widespread debate. If we are still evolving how will we look in the future, and if we are not, then what does that mean? On the genetic level, it would probably be fair to say that human evolution has stopped, but human evolution is not a purely genetic affair and the path of our development as a species cannot be fully understood without an examination of the role played by cultural adaptations. There has been a complex relationship between biological adaptations, such as bipedalism or brain size, and cultural adaptations, such as tool use, since the development of the first stone tools in East Africa around 2.6 million years ago. Stone tools represented a major cultural adaptation that provided our ancestors with the ability to manipulate their environment, a process that led to ever more complex behavioural innovations and one that has continued ever since.

As we saw in chapter 1, our earliest hominin ancestors were very different in appearance to us – if still extant they would look to us very 'ape-like'. This was the case for approximately five million years until the appearance, two million years ago, of *Homo ergaster* – the first human, and the first to rely heavily on cultural adaptations rather than biological ones. The process of human evolution from two million years ago onwards has thus been one of relatively small-scale biological changes in tandem with massive and far-reaching cultural development. It was the development of cultural adaptations that provided the basis for our evolutionary success and produced the current genetic pattern that is largely no longer evolving. The use of cultural adaptations, such as fire and clothing, removed the need for biological adaptation and meant that the basic body plan of the genus Homo has remained relatively unchanged.

Although there are of course differences between species such as *Homo ergaster*, the Neanderthals and *Homo sapiens*, the factor that unites us all is the role that cultural innovation has played in allowing a wide range of habitats to be exploited without the need for further biological adaptation. The massive increases in intelligence were in large part fuelled by a change in the biology of the brain. The average *Australopithecus* brain was about 450 cubic centimetres; the brain of the more human *Homo ergaster* was double that: about 1000 cubic centimetres. Then the brain became even larger: 1400 cubic centimetres in Neanderthals and 1350 cubic centimetres in *Homo sapiens*. This extra grey matter provided the raw material for working out a huge range of environmental manipulations and cultural adaptations.

Some would argue with the idea that our genetic evolution has stopped. They would highlight the role of genetic engineering as meaning that we have entered a period of evolutionary dynamism again: a result of being able to tweak our genome, for instance, to remove cancer and other genetic diseases. This is an attractive idea but it overlooks the fact that many of these diseases take hold later in life, long after the moment when a sperm fertilizes an egg and creates a person's genetic make-up, and as such could be argued to be relatively selectively neutral. Simply put, genetic pre-disposition to heart disease is not the same as heart disease, for which other environmental factors play a major part! Ultimately, genetic engineering is also an example of cultural evolution which continues to play a crucial role in the development of the human species. The pace of cultural adaptation is moving rapidly and producing a greater range of variation than at any other time in our evolutionary history. We may be heading for a homogeneous genetic future but the human evolutionary story tells us that our culture will continue to evolve and flourish as long as humans are around.

A major part of human adaptation is the characteristic ability of our species to live in a wide variety of habitats without any obvious problems. This is partly due to various sorts of cultural adaptation, but biological adaptations also occur along a range, reducing the stress or improving the adaptive capacity of the physiological system as needed. This basic biological flexibility involves how genes are expressed, meaning that the phenotype is responsive and can make some function of the organism or a larger population better suited to a specific environment. In fact, adaptability itself may be regarded as a human adaptation – that is, humans have adapted the ability to respond and adjust to changing environmental conditions across the evolutionary timescale. Reviewing the way in which the human body responds to three environmental conditions – extreme heat, extreme cold, and extreme altitude – reveals a great deal about the uniformity of our species as a result of our shared evolutionary past, but it also vividly illustrates the importance of cultural adaptation or cultural solutions to the problems faced by human populations colonizing new habitats.

First, different hot environments (whether humid or dry) lead to different combinations of responses, so for example, in a humid environment there is little potential for sweating – just as a body in a hot bath cannot expel sweat – and this is where heat stroke is most common. The general response is the same, however: cooling the body. This is necessary to maintain the core body temperature (CBT) of 37°C, the optimum for internal biochemical processes such as enzyme activity, and to prevent loss of consciousness or death by heat exhaustion (at around 40°C to 42°C). In most cases the onset is acute and leads to immediate loss of consciousness and convulsions. A vicious circle is established since this rise of body temperature forces the metabolism to rise and the associated heat production to increase. Hypotension and circulatory failure reduce blood flow and heat transport to the skin and thus reduce heat loss. The circulatory shock impairs renal and hepatic function and damages the central nervous system. Physiological responses are triggered and controlled by temperature-sensitive cells in the anterior hypothalamus, which receive blood from the carotid artery (the vessel through which blood passes to the brain). The brain requires a constant temperature of 37°C to operate, and is threatened by temperatures exceeding 41°C.

Humans are remarkably ineffective at extremes of cold temperatures. Manipulative and motor skills are lost quite rapidly, followed by cognitive abilities, with loss of consciousness at between 31°C to 29°C. Maintaining a high CBT obviously prevents these problems but also allows occupation of temperate habitats: although wasteful, warm-bloodedness allows mammals to live in cold climates. Human adaptations to cold stress are significantly unlike those of other animals, because humans have a very low tolerance to cold stress (in the absence of significant surface insulation such as fur and body hair or very thick subcutaneous fat). People have recovered from serious cases of cold stress, however; they have been known to return to full health having experienced core temperatures 10°C below normal. The average adult should be able to tolerate temperatures close to freezing for up to eight or ten hours without clothing. This may be because of their capacity to generate heat during physical activity. In fact, hypothermic states have been induced in individuals during surgery (particularly of the brain and heart), since blood flow is markedly reduced and heart rate drops significantly. However, hypothermia, when the CBT falls below 35°C, can be fatal and death is likely if CBT falls below 25°C. As with increased thermal stress, a decrease in core body temperature (associated with increased cold stress) is detected by the anterior hypothalamus (as well as cold receptors in the cutaneous tissue). However, responses to cold stress are controlled by the posterior hypothalamus.

At altitude the principle phenomenon to affect humans is a reduction in oxygen (O_2) concentration in the breathable air – in other words, the air is 'thinner'. This makes respiration laboured and work difficult, because the blood is unable to deliver sufficient oxygen for tissues and organs to respire properly. Under normal circumstances, human haemoglobin (a substance in red blood cells that carries oxygen around the body) is ninety-seven percent saturated with oxygen, but this diminishes with altitude. When tissues and organs do not have enough oxygen, they suffer from a condition known as *hypoxia*, which is associated with altitude sickness. For example, at five thousand metres altitude atmospheric pressure is half that at sea level, making it more difficult to get oxygen.

Humans are able to adjust to low oxygen levels through a number of physiological responses (See Table 4.1) controlled by the lower half of the brainstem, called the *medulla oblongata*, which is responsible for most automatic functions of life: respiration, heart function and blood pressure, swallowing, vomiting, sneezing, and coughing (the *medulla oblongata* is an ancient part of the brain – it developed first in fishes around five hundred million years ago). When oxygen levels in the body are low, receptors in the heart's arteries detect changes in blood chemistry – especially high levels of carbon dioxide, the poisonous gas that is a waste product of the body's respiratory system. When carbon dioxide levels increase, oxygen levels decrease, a condition known as *hypercapnia*.

In general, the physiological mechanisms displayed by humans are uniform throughout all populations of the world. Even in different climates everyone responds in the same way to similar stimuli. Thus, the genetic material required for physiological regulation to thermal stress or low oxygen levels is present in every human being, and responses will occur reasonably quickly once an individual is put into a stressful situation (such as a hot or cold environment). Indeed, the number of sweat glands found upon individuals is relatively uniform in all societies, although heat exposure during infanthood determines the number of eccrine glands activated (which represents acclimatization).

So, as a species, humans have largely uniform genetic adaptations, but their adaptability means they physiologically respond differently in different environments.

The uniform genetic adaptations suggest that heat adaptation is an old one. It is likely that adaptation to heat load may be one of the oldest human climatic adaptations, since the origins of the species *Homo sapiens* are believed to be in the hot climate of southern and East African grasslands. The fact that humans are so successful at adapting to different thermal loads further supports heat adaptation as being ancient, and the relative ability to acclimatize to heat stress as opposed to cold stress also suggests a tropical origin of the species. Non-human primates do not share the climatic adaptations possessed by people, despite occupying some of the same habitats. For example, a resting human can tolerate full solar radiation and temperatures up to 50°C, but with much less effective eccrine glands other species can only tolerate significantly lower temperatures. Clearly, climatic adaptation varies between species, and not just according to habitats.

Although many physiological adaptations are uniform among different human populations some extreme physiological responses exist. These demonstrate an important feature of physiological control, which is the ability to acclimatize, or adapt through time. Although all humans have an equal ability to adapt, there may be a time lag between exposure to a stimulus and adaptation to it. Some populations are clearly better adapted to extreme conditions because they have had longer to acclimatize to them. Although physiological differences do occur between groups and individuals, these differences would not be present if successive generations of individuals occupied the same environment. In some instances, full acclimatization may require genetic changes, for instance, during the Korean War it was common for American soldiers to suffer from extremity cooling. Those with a European background were better adapted to this cold stress, and as such suffered fewer incidents of frostbite than the black

Afro-American soldiers who were not adapted to the cold extreme, and suffered more incidents of frostbite.

The adaptation is assumed to be genetic, occurring within human populations after dispersal out of Africa of the ancestral European population. However, after sufficient generations of exposure, all lineages are expected to have the ability to adapt to climatic extremes. Combined with our remarkable ability culturally to adapt to new environments this shows how the human biological adaptation of 'adaptability' has played such an important role in shaping who we are and how we can do what we do in so many different places and in so many ways.

Table 4.1 Human responses to hot, cold, and altitudinous environments

Physiological Responses

Heat	Cold	Altitude
Widening of peripheral blood vessels (vasodilation)	Goose bumps (horripilation)	Increased respiratory rate (hyperventilation) & volume
Increased heart beat & blood flow	Narrowing of the larger arteries & blood vessels (vasoconstriction)	Increased heart beat & blood flow
Sweating	Hormonal secretion	Blood diversion
	Shivering	More acidic blood (respiratory alkalosis)
	Hunger	

Evolutionary Responses

Loss of body hair		
Higher number of eccrine glands		
Bipedalism		

Social and cultural constructions of nature

Today, many of us live in *artificially* constructed environments that may seem to have little to do directly with human adaptation. We spend much our life in buildings, travelling from one to another along city streets in motor-powered vehicles. If we feel cold, we turn up the heating; if we want to speak to a friend in another place, we pick up a phone. Life seems under control – until a storm brings down power lines, or a volcanic eruption interferes with the air travel we had planned. Suddenly we become aware of the greater forces that form part of that environment. Reports of *tsunami* in places where we might go for holidays are particularly hocking, especially when we can watch people lose their lives and homes on live television.

These events make news partly because we expect to have pleasant associations with *nature*, but most of our encounters are also highly *constructed*. We enjoy a patch of garden that we have designed and tended to our own satisfaction, or we might go out to a bounded allotment to dig and grow vegetables. At school, we may have joined an outing to visit a working farm to see the organized way in which other parts of our daily meals are produced, and visits to zoos and safari parks can introduce us to some of the wild animals that live out in the wider world. We may also enjoy a trip to the seaside, and walking out to sea along the (beautifully constructed) pier. All these examples are again of highly *controlled environments*, which actually demonstrate clever and more complicated levels of human adaptability.

Perceptions of the natural world are always *culturally constructed*, for they all represent human adaptations to it, but we should also consider the cultural variety. Not everyone has the same sense of trying to control everything, which characterizes the industrialized world, built alongside the cosmology of Western science. Actually, one of the claims of most Indigenous peoples is that human beings form part of the natural world, and each of those peoples expresses the desire to live in harmony with the *place* they claim as their environment in that world. They have learned from generations before them how to sustain a supply of sustenance for life, and their ancestral stories make reference to it. For example, the people we introduced in the previous chapter, named by anthropologists as *hunters and gatherers*, hold a deep knowledge about when and where to find their food. Ideally for their lifestyle, they move about freely within the area they know, harvesting fruits, roots, and berries as they come into season, tracking animals when they are in the area, and 'working' for only as long as it takes to collect and prepare enough to eat. They amass few belongings, and produce little waste.

There are peoples in different parts of the world who still live in an approximation of this situation. Some live in warm climates so they don't need much in the way of clothes and shelter, although they have devised many uses of the resources available for killing animals and preparing food, or for treating sickness. Those who live in colder regions transformed the material world into protection, constructing weather-proof clothing out of animal skins and plant fibres, and devising warm shelters for their homes.

Different peoples have created different responses to the same environment. In the snowy Arctic, for example, the Inuit built enclosed *iglu*s out of great bricks of snow, heating the inside air with an oil burner; other Native Peoples made tents out of animal skins, open at the apex to let out the smoke that rose from their wood fires. Many of these peoples have now been housed by the national governments who have subsumed their lands, but the facilities are not necessarily superior!

Few people live in isolation, however, and land is rarely as free and available as the hunter-gatherer lifestyle would ideally demand. According to a Cree elder, quoted in a museum display in the Canadian Prairies, it is a crazy idea to think that humans

Figure 4.1 Inuit wearing traditional clothing made from animal skins. Only late in the twentieth century did modern fibres replace these forms of clothing as they were so well designed to cope with life in extreme cold.

© H. Mark Weidman Photography / Alamy

can *own* land 'which was there before we came and will be there when we are gone'. The animal herders we discussed in the previous chapter may share the *idea* of land being available, but they will have rather different views of exactly the same areas of land. Their systems of knowledge are about living together with animals, rather than about hunting them, about finding ways to feed their animals, as well as themselves, and about protecting them from predators such as 'wild' animals, neighbouring hunting societies, or even hostile neighbours who might come to steal them. Herders thus do employ a concept of *ownership* of a living part of that natural world – their animals – but the idea of owning *land* only really evolved as people settled down in one place, and began to cultivate areas of it on a regular basis.

Even cultivation does not necessarily coincide with the concept of ownership, as many of the peoples who live in the rain forests of South America practise a system called *slash-and-burn cultivation*, which requires clearing an area for a crop for only a few years, before moving on to allow the forest to regenerate. Even in more permanent agricultural developments, land may be perceived as being owned by a community and families are allowed to work an area for as many generations as they can keep it in good order, but if they neglect it, it could be passed to someone else. Such a system is still practised in Central America, where descendants of the Aztec and Mayan people live, and nowadays farmers may combine work on their communal *ejido* plots with their use of privately-owned land. Many misunderstandings about land have arisen between peoples with different ideas about it; the case of Manhattan Island being 'sold' to early European settlers, who had developed a clear understanding of land ownership, by people who thought, like the Cree elder mentioned above, that they were just allowing its *usufruct* is a particularly notorious case.

The notion of ownership of land spread as societies grew and specialized, so that some members of a community would tend the land while others engaged in activities such as trade or defence. Food took on a value for sale or exchange, and the means of its production – the land – a related value. Today, the concept of land ownership is so widespread that people who still live by other rules find themselves in conflict with big government projects such as dam construction, mining, and logging. During the eighteenth and nineteenth centuries, nations set themselves up all over the globe by seizing ownership of great swathes of land, even if it was already occupied and wars were

Figure 4.2 The Dänojà Zho Cultural Centre in the Yukon tells the ongoing story of the Tr'ondëk Hwëch'in people whose land was overrun during the Klondike gold rush at the end of the nineteenth century. The people moved upriver and conserved their cultural heritage, such as making racks, represented in this building, to hang salmon to dry for winter food. In the past decade, they have achieved a land-sharing settlement with the Canadian government.
Photograph by Joy Hendry

fought to establish the boundaries. The prior inhabitants of such lands have sometimes even found their home territories marked out as 'a wilderness', or a national park, when they may even be forbidden from entering it.

The so-called Bushmen of Botswana provide one case that has been publicized by the world press, through the efforts of Survival International and other charities to help them retrieve their lands from the big game hunters, who were being issued expensive licenses to operate there. This collective name for the peoples of this land was also imposed by outsiders – they have several different names for themselves – and to add insult to injury they were also being employed to help the tourists track their prey. Tourism has caused problems for other Indigenous peoples, such as the Anangu Aboriginal Australians on whose land the extraordinary Uluru, or Ayers Rock, stands. Their request that it should not be climbed is still often ignored, though the tour guides at least transmit the preference of the people and recount Aboriginal stories about the site. There is even a cultural centre nearby that acknowledges the traditional 'owners' (perhaps better considered as 'users') of the land, but the Australian government apparently fears a loss in interest and tourist revenue should they remove the rope that helps visitors ascend the steep face of the rock, despite the fact that several people fall, and some die, each year.

Interestingly, city dwellers often express strong views about the world they perceive to be *natural*; they are concerned about the declining numbers of birds that visit their gardens, about whales and other animal species that appear to be threatened, and generally about human-induced climate change that is said, for example, to be destroying the snow and ice that provide a habitat for polar bears. Some city dwellers buy weekend properties in the country, so that they can get away from time to time to a life they perceive as closer to nature. They may also become actively involved in trying to conserve what they think of *wilderness*, to prevent it from being *developed* by property magnates or industrialists, and to ensure that there is an adequate habitat for their favourite wild animals to survive.

The subject of *nature* itself is also something that has been theorized by several anthropologists, and one of the best known examples is that proposed by Claude Lévi-Strauss that all humans distinguish in some way between *nature* and *culture*, indeed that the distinction is one of the major irresolvable dichotomies that he argued myths and folkloric stories try to mediate. Another famous theory, put forward by the feminist anthropologist Sherry Ortner, is that women are always given a second class place in society because of their closer association through childbirth with *nature*, which is classified as less highly-valued than *culture* with which men associate themselves.

Clearly, the idea of *nature*, as opposed to *culture*, is a very powerful concept, but not everyone agrees that such a universal distinction can be made. Cambridge anthropologist Marilyn Strathern has used ethnographic data to demonstrate that the situation may be much more complicated. She argues that the idea of a universal *nature/culture* dichotomy associated with a *gender* distinction is an expression of Western ideas that have been imposed by anthropologists on the world views of other peoples. She illustrates her argument by describing aspects of the symbolism of the people at her field site of Mount Hagen, in Papua New Guinea, who make rather different distinctions, for example between 'wild' and 'planted'. Women and men may be associated with each of these in different circumstances, and neither is thought to have domination over the other.

Representing the social and spiritual

Two other ways in which our environment is understood and classified by different peoples are to be found in the *material culture* that we craft out of it, and the way that material culture represents a non-material world of spirits and what in English we call supernatural powers. The English language tends to dichotomize art and technology, just as it does nature and culture, so that natural fibres like cotton and silk are starkly distinguished from those described as *synthetic*, such as nylon and polyester, though their primary component, namely oil, has simply been subjected to greater human intervention.

Material goods that directly represent a world that seems *natural* offer an interesting link that not only breaks down the severity of the dichotomy, but opens doors to understanding perceptions of *nature* that also might be held by other peoples. Consider, for example, the paintings of John Constable, which represent an English view of *nature*, very often also depicting some of the social life of the rural English at the time, who appear to fit so neatly into the scenes he creates.

Now, consider the artistic creations of Australian Aboriginal people, which look nothing like nature to Europeans, who may simply buy such work as a pleasant souvenir of a visit to a foreign land. For people who have grown up in an Aboriginal society, the art means much more, and it may make many references to the world that is seen as quite natural to them. A fascinating art exhibition in the National Gallery of Australia not only includes such starkly different 'dotted' and 'cross-hatched' representations of the *natural* world, but also hangs these side by side with European-style depictions of the Australian landscape and works created by settler Australians for whom that landscape was also home, but who did not share any Aboriginal upbringing. The differences in the last are more subtle, but they are certainly there! Visiting an exhibition of astoundingly skilful (realistic) Western painting with an Aboriginal Australian terminated with a revealing comment, when he said 'these paintings are pretty much like photographs.'

Another element of the material culture that people make in different societies is that it may be thought to hold a *spiritual* power. Much of the work of the Māori people in New Zealand is thought of in this way, and when their beautiful wooden carvings travel to an exhibition, for example, special rituals must be held to protect and pacify the spiritual elements which might otherwise bring misfortune. This is another example of ideas relating to misfortune that we considered in chapter 2, and it is also relevant to our consideration of objects of exchange in chapter 3. One of the examples cited by Marcel Mauss in his book *Le Don* is of Māori and Samoan people who hold that the spirit of an object will bring misfortune to those who fail to make a proper return.

This kind of *spiritual* power may not be distinguished from the *natural* world in which it is found by that other English linguistic dichotomy between the *natural* and the *supernatural*, but the two may be held firmly to be part of each other. Many Native American peoples hold ideas about the *sacredness* of the land itself, and a good example can be found in the famous peace pipes they craft from a particular kind of stone. An important quarry has been protected at the aptly named Pipestone National Park in the state of Minnesota, where visitors may even see the craft being practised and ask questions of contemporary Native American peoples about their understanding of this sacred site. The tobacco plant itself is also held to be sacred, and it is burned with sage and sweet-grass for a ceremony, known as smudging, that is held to have purifying powers, among other things.

In his interesting book *Native Science*, the scholar Gregory Cajete argues that the Western science that is widely accepted as universal leaves out two important elements. The first is the degree to which human beings are themselves part of the natural world which they study and interpret, as if they were outside of it; he makes the same argument mentioned above about scientists wanting to control everything, an argument also discussed by the anthropologist Tim Ingold as a *global* view, since we can only think about the world as a globe if we imagine ourselves outside of it. How many of us had a globe as children so that we could learn about our world, but always in this case from an outside point of view?

Cajete's second criticism of science is that it leaves out the spiritual aspects of the universe it studies, so data that might contribute, like dreams and visions, are not really taken seriously.

Some Native American youths learn of their world by going *into* a part of it that is thought to be sacred, and seeking a vision, perhaps by fasting and smoking the sacred pipe, an important material component of this *inner* quest for knowledge about their relationship with the earth to which they belong. Mother Earth has become a name for the natural world that many Indigenous peoples feel that they share, in contrast to *science,* which tries to stand outside.

For now, let us round up this discussion of engaging with nature by pointing out that anthropologists, whether they call themselves 'scientists' or not, take the information people tell them about dreams and visions seriously, and they use it alongside the material representations those people make of their natural worlds to gain an understanding of the systems of *symbolic classification* that underpin their worlds. These are excellent sources of ethnographic data, and although they may sometimes seem difficult to translate into a language that divides nature from technology, and the spiritual world from science, we can probably all find ways to feel the power of the natural world. We just have different ways of expressing it.

5

Personhood

In this chapter and the next, we will turn to examine the *processes* by which human beings *become* the socially defined persons we have outlined so far. First, we consider *personhood*, present some of the possibilities for the very notion of *persons* within a particular society, and see how they relate to others around them. In the next chapter, we will look in detail at the *ritual* ways in which the person is formed and transformed through the life course. In case this all sounds a bit technical, imagine yourself in a public space, such as a bus or a train, surrounded by people going about their lives. Each of you has roles to play. Among you will be parents, children, husbands, wives, bosses, and workers, many playing more than one of those roles, and each responsible for aspects of their lives defined by the role. There will also be a driver, and possibly a guard or conductor, each responsible for all of you while you sit on that bus or train. These are aspects of the *personhood* of the people thrown together for the journey.

In chapter 4, we introduced the idea that nature and the environment are socially and culturally constructed by the systems of classification that peoples impose on their surroundings. In this chapter we will turn to apply similar principles to the construction of the category of *person* within a society. We have also seen the social body we all inhabit, and the diverse ways in which that body is perceived and used. This time, we will turn to examine the place that actions of and on that body help to form the person within it. In other words, we build on the idea that the learning of language converts the biological being that is a newborn baby into a social being, able to use the system of communication, but here we focus on the roles he or she will play and the position(s) they will hold.

Anthropologists have reported a wide variety of possibilities for this process, and we will consider several examples, but another idea that emerges in this context is that we can also learn something of the anthropologist's background by looking at their work. For example, the need to define and explain this concept of a person can probably be traced to the thinking of Western philosophers, and their ideas about the self. An influential study on the subject was made by Marcel Mauss, who in 1938 gave a lecture in which he contrasted the idea of the self (*moi* in his native French) to the idea of the person (*personne*), drawn from the Latin term *persona* for mask or role. In other languages and world views, the distinction may be very different, if it exists at all. Finally then, we will turn our anthropological lens on the philosophical background of anthropologists brought up in this Maussian tradition, and examine some of the assumptions that may lie behind their quest. Don't forget that we can often learn as much about ourselves as students of anthropology as we can about others!

Becoming a person

To address the business of becoming a person with a role in society, let us consider when this is thought to begin, how it may change, and indeed when and whether it ends. In many societies, a naming ceremony for a baby marks a beginning, for a being that can be named has at least a potential social role. The registering of a new life gives that person a legal status, and where written records are kept on file, details of birth and parentage add a social position to the name as part of a family, which can also be traced back through time. In many countries, the child will then acquire a list of entitlements – to afterbirth care, inoculations against disease, schooling, and in a state with a welfare system, health care for life. The right of a child to these benefits can, in some cases, override the role of the parents, who must comply with expectations of the wider society and its laws, or forfeit their own right to care for the child. So a new human being has acquired the legal status of a person with rights, which will also develop into obligations, for example to attend school.

Within a family, a baby may develop an aspect of personhood before it is born, especially now that parents can see an image of the foetus in the mother's womb. However, people have a range of ideas about the time at which the embryo is thought to become a member of society with the right to lead an independent life. Religious ideas may play a part here, related to notions of the existence of a soul or spirit. For example, Roman Catholics are taught that life must be preserved from the moment of conception, whereas some Buddhists have other ideas about when a soul is thought to enter the growing foetus. In ancient Japan, a child had to be born and crying before society granted it the right to be a person with an entitlement to live, and a practice known as *infanticide* was justified as allowing a growing family properly to feed and support a limited number of offspring. These ideas are of course reflected in the degree of tolerance peoples express towards other practices of population control such as contraception and induced abortion.

A completely different point of view is to be found in the Hindu concept of personhood, reported in the influential work of Louis Dumont. He explains that a newborn child is always thought to be a re-born person because of the principle of reincarnation which underlies Hindu thinking. The previous life of the newly born child therefore influences the fate of the person they will become, who will in turn have to think about how their own behaviour will affect their future reincarnations. This cyclical view of life has no clear beginning or end. It has also been described as *sociocentric* for the way in which a person is born as a member of a *caste* which pre-determines fairly clearly the position they will have in society, their profession, and the limited circle of people with whom they can have social inter-actions, from sharing food to marriage.

Another variable feature about the notion of personhood is how it is thought to be lost. In some contemporary views of the world, a person ceases to exist when they die; other bereaved members of the same society may visit the graves of their loved ones for years, talking to them and perhaps consulting them about important issues. In Japan, people consult their deceased relatives and ancestors in this way, although a more orthodox Buddhist view would be to seek the elimination of the self as an escape from the otherwise continuing cycle of reincarnation. Japanese people draw on various religious ideas, notably Shinto, and although their views vary about what happens to the spiritual part of a person after death, widely shared is the notion that they should not be forgotten. Families practice memorial rites at regular intervals in Japan, as also in China, and one colourful custom is to light lanterns for departed relatives and dispatch them down a river in little boats. For the souls of aborted babies, such care is thought to avoid the misfortune that a neglected spirit might bring to living beings. However, after a number of years varying regionally between thirty-three and fifty, Japanese spirits are thought to merge safely into an ancestral 'one' when they will be remembered together instead of as individual persons.

What makes up a person?

How then, according to the views of various peoples, are persons constituted? What are their characteristics, and how can these be identified? Anthropologists have found many possibilities, and it is not even necessary for the category of person to coincide with the physical presence of a human body. The concept of a *cyborg* has been developed recently, and computer games allow us to create multiple persons to live in entirely invented worlds. The film *Avatar* adds a technologically-enabled angle to the idea that several peoples already have, that a spirit can leave the physical body and go travelling. This extends the idea, shared by many religious faiths that a spirit or a soul continues after a person dies. There are also several peoples who attribute personhood to beings other than humans.

For example, we previously mentioned that many Indigenous people speak of Mother Earth, and examining their ideas about the caring, providing role of the earth in their lives offers good ethnographic material to understand how they also think about the person of a mother. In Native North America, the moon may be addressed as Grandmother, and Cree women hold ceremonies which appeal to her as someone capable of interceding on their behalf with their Father, the Creator, thus touching on a role that a grandmother might be expected to play. An interesting sense of corporeality understood in reference to Grandmother Moon was illustrated in a round-robin e-mail that complained about exploratory missiles that were being directed at the body of this *person* to whom women were accustomed to offering prayers.

A person is more than a body, then, and even that category is thought to be built up in various ways. For a group of Malay people with whom Janet Carsten worked on the island of Pulau Langkawi in the Andaman Sea, personhood is inextricably bound up with the contributions of relatives. It is gained gradually throughout life by a process of feeding, and being fed, so the acquisition of personhood, which begins at conception, can only draw close to completion as a person grows through the roles of marriage, parenthood, and even grandparenthood. The concept of the hearth where food is prepared may stand for the whole house in this society, and itself plays a part in the constitution of a person. Substances involved start with the blood a mother is thought to share with her babies in the womb, the milk she feeds to them after they are born, which is itself thought to be made from her blood, and in turn to make their blood, and then later, the rice she cooks for them. These substances play such an important part in this process that a child who is fostered or adopted also becomes a member of the family group with whom sexual relations would be forbidden as incestuous, just as for anyone born into it.

Figure 5.1 South East Asian cooking hearth similar to that described by anthropologist Janet Carsten.
Photograph by Jonathan Spencer

For the Wari' Indians of Western Brazil, studied by American anthropologists Beth Conklin and Lynn Morgan, nourishment is again needed to make a person. In this case, it starts before a child is born, for the combination of a father's semen, which is thought to make the flesh, and a mother's blood, must be made many times during pregnancy to ensure a good, healthy child. Once the child is born, the development of the person continues through breast feeding, but a father still has the role of bringing food for the mother to make into breast milk. In fact, the need for the male contribution is so strong that if a father should die, or disappear, during the mother's pregnancy, another man will be expected to provide the extra nourishment, both of semen before birth and edible food afterwards. A man who has played this role is regarded as related to the child, whoever the initial father was, and this element of the procedure Conklin and Morgan contrast with the value placed on identifying a biological father in the United States, even if he has had nothing to do with the subsequent raising of a child.

Hugh Brody, a British anthropologist and filmmaker, went as a young man to work with the Inuit (formerly known as Eskimo) people who live in snowy northern Canada. He explained his presence among them to be to learn the native language, which he knew was called Inuktitut. The local people, who could also speak English, agreed to help him, and set about the task enthusiastically. He recounts now – many years later – that he found the process to involve much more than studying ways of speaking, as he was soon included in hunting trips, fishing expeditions, and all kinds of other Inuit activities, especially those carried out by men. Some months later, he discovered that the name of the language, *Inuktitut*, literally means 'like an Inuk', and as he had learned that Inuk means 'person', the word for the language in fact constitutes all the things which it takes to make up an Inuk person, in this case a man. What more could an anthropologist ask for, in order to learn as much as possible about the lives of the people he or she has chosen to study?

To gain a clear idea of the constitution of a person in any one society, it is useful to read up about a particular case. Education plays an important part in making a person in any society, and this includes training in the manners and customs of social interaction as well as in activities that prepare for economic life, such as the hunting and fishing of the Inuit, and/or the formal schooling of cities and states. In the Japanese language, cooking metaphors are used to describe a child in the process of becoming a full person, which in this case involves growing up, getting married, and preferably having children. Such a completed person is described as 'one helping of a social person' – *ichininmae no shakaijin*, like a complete plate of food. In contrast, a person who has not reached this ideal stage of personhood may be described as *mada dekiteinai*, or 'not yet done', as for cooked food not ready to be eaten. This second phrase may also be used by parents to apologize to others when their children are misbehaving!

The person in society

The Japanese expression for a complete adult – literally 'one helping' – indicates another aspect of the notion of personhood, namely that persons need to be defined as part of society, 'one helping' suggesting a wider whole of which each person is part. People speaking to each other in Japanese also need to know how they are related within that society so that they can choose appropriate language. A small child is addressed by a personal name for a short while, but once old enough to play with other children relative age dictates the terms to be used. Elders are addressed as 'big brother' or 'big sister', and expected behaviour patterns follow the terms. The terms change with time, but the age distinction continues throughout school life, and in the workplace, where everyone is addressed according to relative age and status position. People are much more likely, therefore, to address one another by title, rather than simply by name, which is why it is so important when opening new business relations in Japanese society to exchange name cards providing this information.

The importance of relationships in defining personhood may be expressed in many different ways. In the two cases we examined for substance of personhood, the kin or family relations were essential to creating a full person, but in the Malay case described by Janet Carsten, the house or hearth is also a vital component. This feature is found widely in the anthropological literature of the area known as Austronesia, which includes the peoples who occupy Pacific Islands, as well as much of East Asia. Hindu weddings include many rituals creating new social ties, but one takes place around a specially created 'hearth' as part of creating a new home for the couple. A person may continue through life to be defined by their house, each member only distinguished further by the role they play within that house. In the case of the Wari', relations with kin are also necessary for making a person, and the early period with the mother is particularly associated with the house, because a child who dies at this stage would be buried under the house. As they grow older, however, Wari' children build up a set of relations outside the house, and they gradually move to become part of the wider community, which will take care of their burial when they die.

We came across the idea that personhood is *sociocentric* when we considered the Hindu caste system, but the role of *person* is related to the wider social system in every society. In the English language, we also have an idea of shared *blood*; for example 'we are blood relatives', or 'he is of blue blood', but the quality of *nurture*, or upbringing, is contrasted with *nature*, and the training and education that nurture implies may open up opportunities for social mobility. As we saw in chapter 3, persons *acquire* status through their birth and family connections, but different societies offer different possibilities for *achieving* status, each of which contributes to a person's total role, and the roles people play need to be part of the classification system of the wider society.

A number of anthropologists have discussed society in terms of the roles people play. The work of the Canadian scholar Erving Goffman, who moved between anthropology and sociology, has been particularly influential. He described what he called the 'presentation of self' in theatrical terms, using words such as 'acting', 'performing' and being 'front' and 'back stage'. He also attributed a high level of self-awareness to the roles we play, and suggested that we manage the impressions we create in order to achieve certain benefits. In a public situation, where we are known for a particular aspect of our person – say as an employee – we need to make a good impression on our employers. As a parent or child, we may have different roles to play; in the first case to elicit appropriate behaviour, probably different for a public 'front stage' venue to 'back stage' at home; in the second, a performance might be designed to secure benefits, such as a special treat or an increase in pocket money!

Norwegian anthropologist Fredrik Barth further developed these ideas, initially working with a fishing crew, each of whom had been allocated particular roles in the boat: catching, sorting, and storing the fish, as well as managing the boat itself. He describes the way crew members played out their roles, even to the point of exaggeration, perhaps to make a good impression on their guest, the anthropologist! Goffman's study was also used by American anthropologist Gerald Berreman to help him interpret contrasting outcomes of work he did in India while using two different assistants. The first was a high-caste Brahmin, and Berreman felt that people he interviewed had been careful to present their behaviour as appropriate to their own caste, even to the point of lying if necessary. The second, appointed only after the first fell ill, was a Muslim, and Berreman found that the same people were much more willing to disclose their actual behaviour, rather than the roles they thought the Brahmin would expect them to play!

Berreman's case raises an important aspect of the care anthropologists need to apply to the study of personhood, for the way that people describe their behaviour, as opposed to how they actually practice it, could well be different. The former might reflect the expectations of the wider society, but be an ideal to which they don't always manage to conform. An anthropologist thus needs to be aware of this distinction, and compare reports of behaviour with their own observations, as well as taking into account descriptions given to them by people of how they *should* behave under certain circumstances. In other words, they need to compare what people *do* with what they *say* they do, and what they say they *should* do. The full range of variety here in any one situation may take an anthropologist quite a long time to work out, and this is one of the reasons why they like to spend a year or more in the field.

At the beginning of this chapter, we mentioned an essay by Marcel Mauss about the notions of 'person' and 'self'. That essay also used metaphors based on the theatre to describe the roles people play in society, as distinct from the 'self' who plays those roles. Mauss emphasized the importance of naming in identifying aspects of these roles, and offered examples of some peoples who have a limited stock of names to be allocated to particular persons in their society who are expected to play those roles. We can compare such a system of names with the titles people acquire through education, like 'Doctor', 'Reverend', or 'Professor', or through election, like 'Councillor', 'Member of Parliament', or 'President'.

Mauss also noted that in some societies people are given several names, each of which marks out different roles they play at different times, such as when a person acts as a child to his or her parents, while at school the same child is a pupil, a good musician, or perhaps a football captain. Later in life, the same person might become a husband or wife, at the same time as carrying out different roles at work and play, and then return home to be a parent to his or her own child. In the English language, we allocate different names to the roles we play at different moments, and a husband might refer to his wife as Mum in front of the children, but by her first name – or a nickname – when they are alone. At work, the same woman may be known more formally, say, as Ms Smith or Dr Smith.

Mauss didn't make these parallels to everyday life in his own society, it should be noted; he saw the practices he described as characteristic of *other* peoples, whom he sometimes describes as 'primitive', in contrast to the way that Europeans are able to identify and distinguish their individual self (*moi*), as separable from the notion of person (*personne*). This ability he dates only to the thinking of philosophers of the Enlightenment, who proposed to have discovered rational thought, as opposed to the acceptance of doctrines imposed on us by institutions such as the Church. Among these was René Descartes whose idea that the concept of mind, or consciousness, could be separated from the body, became known as Cartesian dualism. Many other philosophers have contributed to thinking about the individual self, as an autonomous person who needs to be responsible for his or her own behaviour, and Mauss mentioned in this context the work of the German thinker Immanuel Kant.

It was towards the end of this period that anthropology was conceived, along with other disciplines such as psychology, whose famous protagonist, Sigmund Freud, popularized the concept of the *ego,* which has entered our language in terms such as 'egotistical' to emphasize again the idea of individual autonomy. In fact, both the concept of the *self* and that of the *ego* are socially constructed, like any other idea of the *person*, and we can trace their development to scholars of the time. They thus contribute in no small way to the system of classification that underpins the thinking of anthropologists raised in that world, and to their interest in this notion of the person that has formed the subject matter of this chapter. The idea of the individual has played such an important part in 'Western thought' that it has even been called a 'cult of the individual', perhaps thereby seen as an alternative 'religion' to the teachings of the Church.

The origins of personhood

It is something of an irony that one of the key facets of humanity – personhood – is tantalizingly hard to identify in the deep time frame of human evolutionary history. What we can see often comes from glimpses of human-like behaviours in our ancestors and through comparative study of our close primate cousins. The identification of evidence of personhood within human evolutionary development presents an intriguing challenge because of the scarcity of data with which we often have to work.

Figure 5.2 Cast reconstructions of fossil skulls created for study by biological anthropologists. Left – *Homo neanderthalensis*, Middle – *Homo floresiensis* & Right – *Homo sapiens*.

Certainly by the time we reach our own species *Homo sapiens* we can easily see material evidence for personhood, from complex grave goods to the painting of individual handprints on cave walls from Europe to South America. But what about earlier species of hominin? Can we see evidence of the concept of personhood? Moving further afield, what can we learn from our closest primate cousins, the chimpanzees, about identity and recognition of self?

As for when we can begin to identify self in the evolutionary record, the answer is not a simple one, but we can start by looking for evidence of ritual behaviour (which will be discussed in more detail in the next chapter). If we use a very broad definition of ritual (such as any non-subsistence related behaviour), then we can perhaps see some indication of relevant activities in *Homo heidelbergensis* from five hundred thousand years ago. A species of hominin that was directly ancestral both to us and to the Neanderthals, *Homo heidelbergensis* was a large-brained hunter who manufactured complex weaponry in the form of stone tools and spears. They were capable of bringing down very large prey species and evidence, in the form of large numbers of pristine stone tools left lying unused on the ground, at the site of Boxgrove in the South of England, has been interpreted by some as a ritualized behaviour. Similarly, at the site of Schöningen in Germany, dated to four hundred thousand years ago, pristine spears have been excavated in association with buried horse bones. While it is not possible to state definitively that this is evidence of personhood or identity in the evolutionary past it is certainly suggestive of such, and is recognizably human.

When we consider the Neanderthals, we are faced with a much wider range of evidence for behaviours that clearly point towards a concept of self. The Neanderthals buried their dead, wore clothes, made jewellery, and recent evidence has suggested that they may even have worn makeup made from rock pigments. Ultimately, we are limited by what we can recognize as evidence of personhood in the evolutionary record; it is quite likely that early hominins had some sense of their own existence but we cannot see evidence for this until we reach the much later human hominins. Personhood is something we generally associate with being strictly human, but the evolutionary record offers us intriguing glimpses of personhood in the past.

One of the clearest indications of the concept of the individual and group we have from our evolutionary past is the appearance of intentional burial in the archaeological record. Fossil skeletons are distinct from intentionally buried skeletons because of the way in which they were deposited. Fossils are best thought of as accidents of preservation that leave behind a record only under the most fortuitous of circumstances. Conversely, an intentionally buried body has a much higher chance of preservation because it is placed in a pre-prepared hole in the ground. Here though, we must again sound a note of caution – just because a body was intentionally placed in a hole in the ground does not necessarily mean it was buried in the same way that we understand the concept. In the past, our hunter-gatherer ancestors may have buried their dead in order to prevent attracting predators or simply to stop a much-used site from becoming smelly and spoiled by the rotting remains of Uncle Ugg in the corner.

The earliest intentional burials (in the broad sense of a body being placed in a dug grave) are actually found among the Neanderthals and date from around seventy thousand years ago, but there is much debate as to intentionality. The first *Homo sapiens* burial comes from a site in Southern Australia called Lake Mungo and dates to around sixty thousand years ago, although some researchers argue that intentional burial may have been practiced by *Homo heidelbergensis* as far back as half a million years ago.

What then of our primate cousins? Intelligence and problem-solving abilities have been widely recorded in a large number of primates but can we equate this with a sense of personhood? The tempting answer would be simply to say no, and to allow only humans this concept. But as ever in biological anthropology the data is less clear cut. We can use a concept called *theory of mind* to determine if an animal is self-aware. To possess theory of mind means that an animal understands that its own thoughts can differ from others. The classic test with primates is to paint a red dot on their head and then show them a mirror – if they touch the mirror it suggests that they do not recognize themselves but if they touch the red dot on their head it suggests they are self-aware and are said to possess theory of mind. Chimpanzees pass this test and furthermore have demonstrated that they can determine what another chimpanzee will think based on observation and forethought – a startlingly human-like behaviour. The primatologist Frans de Waal even recorded two male chimpanzees recognizing a former alpha male they had killed during a take-over of the group, in a video beamed on to the wall of their enclosure, and becoming alarmed at the thought that he was back from the dead.

6

Ritual, ceremony, and identity

Ritual and ceremony form one of the most fascinating and enlightening aspects of anthropology. We touched on elements of the subject when we discussed the way symbolism is used as a means of communication within a specific society, and here we will see the importance of its role again. Rituals and ceremonies are also among the most public of events in social life, and anthropologists are often allowed, or even invited to participate, so they offer a good opportunity for collecting information. Rituals are full of symbolism – indeed, a symbol might be considered the smallest unit of ritual – and discussing them often leads to a much deeper understanding of society than any number of conversations about everyday life.

So first, what is ritual? Several definitions have been offered by different anthropologists, and each has validity, sometimes particularly appropriate to the society where they worked, or perhaps to some prior understanding of their own (we must be vigilant about our own expectations when we work in other societies). In all cases, however, a ritual event involves *behaviour prescribed by society*, and this can be a minimal working definition. Participants must also observe conventions that are agreed to be appropriate by the others who take part, or the event will not be deemed to have achieved its aim. Some of the definitions also suggest the need for a religious element, or the involvement of a spiritual power, but as we shall see, this is not always easy to identify, especially in a society where some have rejected the very idea of religion.

Rites of passage

The rituals most relevant to becoming a person in society, and acquiring an identity within a social group, are those that have been termed *rites of passage*, in other words those that mark the passage of an individual, or a group of age-mates, through the various stages of life set out in the local system of classification. In different societies, these rites take place at different points, but another French scholar by the name of Arnold van Gennep noticed that the rites have similar characteristics wherever and whenever they are found. He compared society to a house with different rooms, each of which can be seen as an important category within that society – youth, warrior, adult, old person – and in order to pass successfully from one room to another, it is necessary to carry out ritual activities. Van Gennep noticed that the rituals themselves can be divided into three stages, as follows:

1. **Rites of Separation**, or **Preliminal Rites:** separate the participants from their previous roles; use symbols of death.
2. **Rites of Transition**, or **Liminal Rites:** may involve a period apart from society.
3. **Rites of Incorporation**, or **post-Liminal Rites:** integrate the participants into the new stage; use symbols of rebirth and regeneration.

Van Gennep's book *Rites of Passage*, which was first published in 1909, has stood the test of time. In it he offers numerous rites of passage, which he clusters around events such as pregnancy and childbirth, thus marking the start of life, initiation into adulthood or other important groups, marriage, and death, so the end of life, that may also be expressing the start of something new. He also discusses territorial rites, a topic we will examine in the next chapter, when we look at belonging and the marking of boundaries around social groups. There are also rites that mark the passage of time.

The rites associated with pregnancy and childbirth are sometimes closely related to those associated with weddings, because in many societies a marriage is not thought to be complete until at least one child has been born. In Japan, for example, the celebration associated with a first child links the two sets of grandparents through the flesh of the newborn child, and their new relationship is called *nikushin*, or flesh relation. It is a little like the British custom of keeping the top layer of a three-layer wedding cake for the christening, or other kind of naming ceremony, so that the marriage is seen to be fertile. Many wedding celebrations around the world include reference to the activities of the first night, which may even be part of the nuptial rituals, followed by a ceremonial checking of the bedclothes for evidence that the bride was a virgin. Otherwise the honeymoon, which is customary in many parts of the world, is usually a literal separation of the couple – a liminal, transition stage – from the rest of the family.

Once a woman is deemed to be pregnant, there are many ceremonies in different societies which mark the start of a period of transition, as van Gennep calls it. The English term, confinement, even expresses the idea of being 'confined' to the house, or some other inner place. These days most expectant mothers in the English-speaking world go out and about during their pregnancy, but there are many societies where there is, or was in the past, a practice of separating pregnant and even menstruating women from the wider society. Anita Diamant's novel *The Red Tent* is precisely about this practice among biblical characters such as Dinah, daughter of Jacob and sister of Joseph, and she gives much detail about how she believes they cared for one another in their red tent, especially at the time of childbirth. From the perspective of the men of such a society, women may be regarded as polluting at these times, which justifies their separation – and coincidentally – removes them from preparing food and their other normal work! Judith Okely provides a detailed explanation of such practice for the Traveller–Gypsies in England.

The birth of a child marks the beginning of rituals to welcome this new person into society, at the same time as reintegrating the mother into everyday life. There is often a period of adjustment during which the mother adapts to her new role, which is another example of a transition, or liminal state. The umbilical cord may be given special attention, for example by being ceremonially buried, and the place chosen may be significant. We saw how the Wari' will bury a baby who dies under the house, which is also where the umbilical cord goes. In Japan, too, it has been customary to bury a boy's cord in the garden, as he is supposed to stay and inherit the home, while a girl's is kept in a special box that she can take with her when she leaves home to marry.

A naming ceremony may mark the start of personhood, as discussed, and the study of names and ceremonies associated with them can provide much information about relations established at such a time. As Marcel Mauss pointed out, some societies have a fixed stock of names, and new members will be given the name of someone who has recently died. A similar practice is found in many societies, where links to previous generations are marked by the choice of at least a second name, and surnames like McDonald and O'Flynn indicate 'the son of' used in this way in Scotland and Ireland in the past. In other societies, a name need not be chosen until a later rite of passage, and a child may simply be referred to as the son or daughter of the family for several years.

Whether a name is involved or not, the general purpose of these early ceremonies is to introduce a new being into the social group, and those who are related to the child in some way are expected to attend. The child may be given a special garment to wear, special food will be served, and photographs will be taken to mark the occasion. There is often a religious service, and gifts will be presented to the child by his or her new relations. These aspects of the ceremony – clothes, food, gifts – are common to other occasions in the process of turning that biological being into a fully-fledged social one, along with those appropriate to the specific occasion. For children, there may be celebrations of a first outing, first solid food, first teeth, first haircut, first school, first holy communion, first hunting success, first fish caught – in all these cases, anthropologists can examine local practices to learn about the system of classification and the values of that particular society.

Van Gennep has a long and relevant chapter in his book about rites of initiation, which can include rites of entry into age grades and adulthood, as well as into particular groups such as a profession,

Figure 6.1 Ritual for a baby eating his first solid food in Japan. Photograph by Yukiko Shimizu

or a religious sect. The period of transition may be quite long, with time for education or training in skills required for full membership in the group. Initiates may live outside society for this time, allowed to behave in ways that are normally unacceptable, as we have seen in the case of Maasai entry into adulthood. They have to root around for food, and take care of themselves, while their hair is allowed to become unkempt. The shaving of their heads, which are then painted with ochre, is part of the ceremony of incorporation into their new adult status. A parallel custom for Athapaskan girls in the Northern Yukon takes place at first menses, when they build a tent and stay out in it until they have perfected various adult feminine tasks.

This time 'in the bush' is supposed to be something of an ordeal, which is another common feature of initiation rites in many societies. Scarification of the body, a painful process that leaves a permanent mark, may take place as part of this ritual. However, it may be administered after a period of intense loneliness, or inactivity, so that a person undergoes the pain as part of their welcome return to normal life, with a newly acquired status. Similarly, Native American youths practice a period of separation in order to seek a vision, and this is accompanied by fasting, which triggers an altered consciousness. In Western societies, some sporting clubs hold initiation rituals that involve imbibing a great deal of alcohol, another way of altering consciousness, and apparently subjecting the new recruit to considerable humiliation.

A good study of initiation rituals is to be found in *Initiation,* edited by Jean La Fontaine, and a detailed analysis of some of the symbolism involved in a couple of studies is made by Victor Turner in *The Forest of Symbols* and *The Ritual Process.*

Many Indigenous peoples have been forbidden from practising rituals that appear to be cruel and painful by the colonizing powers that built nations around them. At the same time, those 'modern' industrial societies do not seem to have found a rite of passage that ensures full entry into adulthood, while social commentators complain that adolescence extends into the twenties and sometimes beyond. Organizations like the scouting and guiding movements offer exciting ways for youngsters to learn to fend for themselves away from home, and there are those who seek tattoos and piercings when they become old enough to make independent decisions about their bodies, but a fully sanctioned set of ceremonies seems to be lacking. Sometimes parents will organize parties for special birthdays, such as the eighteenth or twenty-first, but the age varies even within the same society, and again in different countries. The British writer Geoffrey Ben-Nathan, who feels that a complete rite of passage would help young people to find more fulfilled lives, has put his ideas into a book entitled *"I'm Adult! Aren't I!"*:

Figure 6.2 Two British youths carrying out part of their National Citizen Service, activities proposed as a rite of passage into adulthood in the UK.
UK Department of Education, Young People Division

Understanding Juvenile Delinquency and Creating Adults Out of Children – The Case for a Formal Rite of Passage, and he is working with the British government to introduce such a rite.

Wedding ceremonies are often the next important rite of passage for a young person, and these complete the transition to adulthood in many societies. The symbolism associated with creating a marital bond usually expresses rather clear ideas about kinship and families, for the ceremony is either ensuring the continuity of an existing family line, or creating a new unit. This is a crucial and dangerous stage of crossing categories (or van Gennep's rooms) for it involves at least two persons redefining themselves, as well as adjustments between their own kin, and the rituals are correspondingly elaborate. They may start with ceremonies of betrothal, when the arrangement for the marriage is sanctioned by the families involved, and this will be followed by a period of preparations on either side, before the actual wedding itself. The American engagement shower is one example.

Rites of separation are usually a fun part of the proceedings since it is a last chance for the youngsters to get together with their friends before they become attached. Hen parties and stag nights have become popular in many Western countries, and the opportunities for dressing up and fooling around seem to be invented anew every year in the UK these days. In Mexico, girls dress up as the main characters in the wedding to come, at a *despedida de soltera* (seeing off spinsterhood), and their enactments may include a full play of the likely expectations of the husband-to-be on the wedding night! In Scotland, a groom may be dispatched by his friends on a passing truck, as if to protect him from the life to come, but the driver will usually bring him safely back after a trip around the block!

Exchanges of gifts usually form part of the marriage proceedings, and these may be quite substantial, as a wedding gift can be a kind of settlement for the future in the case of a non-inheriting child. Arranging a good marriage for a daughter is a way of ensuring her future when she is expected to leave home, and building up a *dowry* or *trousseau* can help to make a good match in many societies. There is also a custom of *bridewealth*, which was misunderstood sometimes as a payment for a bride, but is often just one in a series of economic exchanges that cement and validate a union between two descent groups, through the marriage of their members. This is the situation Monica Wilson raised when she said that cattle are driven 'down the path of human relations'. Anthropologists can make a good map of the social relations being set up when they look at the exchanges that take place at the time of a wedding, and this is also an excellent way to see in material form some of the expectations for the lives of the participants.

The last series of rites of passage are those associated with death. Like the ones for weddings and childbirth, they may be spread over a longish period as the death of one person is just the beginning of a period of mourning for the bereaved. This period may coincide with that of a journey into the afterlife thought to be made by the soul or spirit of the one who has died. This time, the rites of separation are the most marked of the three stages, for the symbolism of death is accurately representing the situation, and there will be various ways in which those remaining behind can mark their farewells: incense is lit in Japan, a handful of earth is sprinkled into the grave at Christian funerals, and a big funeral pyre is built in India. The period of transition may involve activities associated with realigning the social group, alongside offering prayers and other rites for the safe passage of the deceased. The rites of incorporation allow the bereaved kin to return to a new life without the person who has left them.

In some places, memorial rites continue for many years, and there may even be a second burial, to create a final resting place once the interim rites are complete. Many people continue to visit the graves of their departed kin at regular intervals after they have died, presenting flowers or discussing continuing issues with a long-term partner. Elsewhere, there might be a family altar at home to remember those who have died, with graves visited only on special occasions. In Japan, for instance, one family member inherits the obligation to look after a household Buddhist altar where the ancestors are remembered, individually for a period of fifty or sixty years and then collectively with other ancestors who went before them. A portion of the first rice of the day is usually offered there, as well as occasional pieces of fruit, or a bottle of something that the most recently deceased member

Figure 6.3 Buddhist altar kept in a Japanese home.
Photograph by Joy Hendry

liked to drink. Once a year, a more elaborate ceremony is held, and family members who live far away will return to offer incense and remember their parents or grandparents. Sometimes such visitors go to the Buddhist altar before they greet their living relatives, and some families hold important discussions in front of the open doors of the altar. Many people also put recently received gifts in front of the altar before they open them. The departed members of the family are still very much present, and this is one of the reasons why misfortune may be attributed to the souls of people who have no one to carry out these rites.

The ritualization of gender and sexuality

So far we have discussed rites of passage in general terms, without paying much attention to the gender of the participants, although there are often quite stark differences. This is because one of the roles of the rites is precisely to construct gender differences, which form an important element of the changes in age and status. When a baby is born, the sex is usually the first thing to be announced, all other things being well, and somewhat ironically, this has become such an important part of the birth announcement that couples may ask not to be told the sex of their baby even though a scan during pregnancy can reveal this information quite easily.

This biological detail is just the beginning of a lifelong process, however. Like all the other social aspects of personhood, gender must be learned, and boys and girls are socialized to play the appropriate roles in their society. The distinct colours of baby garments – pink for girls and blue for boys – make an early mark, although these vary in different countries. Gifts are different, too, and may indicate expectations of the roles to be played, as noted above for the location of the umbilical cord. Garments worn for a baby's first shrine visit in Japan indicate the same expectation as a boy is wrapped in a black kimono bearing the family crest, whereas a girl wears bright colours, celebratory hues that she will also wear on her wedding day. Only when she joins a ceremony as a mother, or grandmother, will she indicate her permanent family membership by wearing a black kimono with the family crest.

The treatment and training of boys and girls is also often very different from an early age, even when people claim they will make no distinction. Japanese children have to take off their shoes when they enter the home, and while boys tend to leave their footwear in disarray, girls are expected to tidy into pairs not only their own, but those of boys who may be entering at the same time. The Gypsy girls that Judith Okely describes are taught from an early age to sit with their legs together, and to keep their washing separate from that of their fathers and brothers. Girls in some societies may be dressed in jeans, pretty much as their brothers are, but it would be highly unusual for a boy to be sent out in a dress. In Islamic societies where adults are strictly separated, girls are allowed to be fairly free until they approach puberty, although they may well be given more household tasks, while boys will learn to do the things that men take care of, usually outside the home.

Puberty rituals are clearly associated with the time when gender differences connect most directly with developing sexuality, and the distinct roles that children have been learning may be honed at this stage. The Athapaskan puberty rite mentioned in the last section literally tested feminine skills such as food preparation and sewing, and although other female members of the family would visit the girl in the bush to see how she was getting along, the teaching would mostly have been done by this time. The components of the symbolism are different, but much of the meaning is parallel to the rituals for girls described by Audrey Richards, Victor Turner, and other African specialists.

After puberty, women and men in many societies are expected to live differently, although the explanations for these distinctions again vary from one society to another. In Mexico, it is said that a man would be unable to control his sexual desires if he found himself alone with an unrelated woman, so a situation such as this is to be avoided by whatever means available. Various explanations have been put forward for why Muslim women wear veils or a burqa, but the Moroccan sociologist Fatima Mernissi has argued convincingly that they provide power and protection against men who are again thought to lack control if they see too much of an unrelated woman. The bodies of the Gypsy women, described by Judith Okely, are said to be highly polluting for men, which is why they must keep their legs together, wash their clothes separately, and generally wear rather loose, cover-all clothing. When they are cooking, they wear aprons which are said to protect the food, rather than their clothes!

In practice, there may again be some considerable difference between stated ideas and the way people actually behave. Okely, for example, points up a paradox between the descriptions Gypsy men give of their protected women and the power those same women in fact need to do their work. This situation is related to fears Gypsies hold about the mainstream, or *gorgio* people, who are also thought to be polluting, but with whom contact is required (by their women) to make a living out of dealings with them. In Japan, women act very deferentially towards men, often strategically, which fools many a casual foreign observer, and there is some good ethnography demonstrating the power these women wield over men in practice. Here is another important role for anthropology then, for it is only long-term study of language and society that allows a researcher to get behind the immediate impressions.

Much anthropology nowadays focuses specifically on women, and often this is done by female anthropologists who, for a while, complained that the literature tended to favour the lives of the men in any society, especially on questions of power and politics. Annette Wiener, as we saw, put the balance right in the understanding of the Trobriand Islands after Bronisław Malinowski's work. Oxford couple Edwin and Shirley Ardener worked together in Cameroon, and although Edwin was the only one to hold an official position at Oxford University at the time, Shirley orchestrated the editing and publication of many books focusing on the perspective of women. She later set up a Centre for Cross-Cultural Studies on Women (now the International Gender Studies Centre), which has become very successful. Her work includes a wonderful paper about the power of women who use their sexuality, by raising their skirts, to frighten off marauding men, but Edwin also published an influential paper on the way that the language of women was undervalued, or 'muted'.

Like the Centre, more recent studies use the word *gender*, to emphasize the socially constructed nature of sexuality, and to allow the representation of masculinity, alongside the feminist studies of women that burgeoned for a while. They also include transgender as a subject, and the situation of homosexuals and others whose lives go beyond the male/female dichotomy that dominated the earlier work. In some societies, from an early age people may be allocated roles that cross the male-female divide, and they will have a special part to play, particularly in rituals. In India, for example, a group known as the *hijra*, who describe themselves as a third gender, may turn up at weddings and birth celebrations to dance, wish the participants well, and of course, receive money. Their liminal position (neither one thing nor the other – they are usually biologically classed as eunuchs) gives them the power to bless, but also to curse should they be ignored.

Homosexuality has become the focus of quite a lot of anthropological work in recent years, sometimes associated with the concept of liminality, as in the case of the hijra, but not always distinguished from heterosexuality in any one individual, who may practice both. This is known as bisexuality in English, but in historical Japan, for example, men in positions of power are reported to have called for a girl or a boy to come to them, as the mood took them. This raises the subject of sexual activity for play, more commonly interpreted as men exploiting women, who are seen to be practising 'the oldest profession', but in Japan, too, there are places, known as 'host clubs', where women may go to play, just as men do in hostess clubs. This is, of course, also the country in which the famous *geisha* are said to practice an art that takes years of training, and no small degree of ritual. Here again, anthropology teaches us not to impose our own categories on the activities of others.

Creating an identity

All the ritual activity we have considered thus far contributes to the formation of a person's identity or identities within the social world they inhabit. There are essentially two parts to this identity: the first is allocated to them by society, usually according to the structural positions they occupy as they pass through van Gennep's 'rooms'; and the second an identity which they choose for themselves by their own actions, or *agency*, as the anthropological term describes it. This identity will approximate the playing out of personhood, and the distinction between the two parts also reflects the distinction between *ascribed* and *achieved* status. Identity may also be adjusted according to the situation, as in the presentation of self.

Various resources are brought into play when people create an identity for themselves, and the same person will draw on different aspects of their resources in the different situations they encounter. *Place* is probably the strongest source of identity for most people: the place they were born, the place they live, and the place with which they identify through their parents and kin group.

If each of these places is the same, then there may not be an issue of identity unless and until they move away, or travel far enough to look at their place from an outside perspective. If the place of birth is different from the place of residence and different again from the place or places with which their parents associate, then an element of choice enters into the building of identity. One or other of the possibilities may be chosen strategically according to the value such places are given by people they meet, or to build common ground. There is also the possibility of choosing to identify with one parent or ancestor rather than others for reasons of social acceptability or convenience.

At this point, an understanding of history, their own and that of their potential associates, may contribute to the decision. For example, Indigenous peoples of a mixed background may have hidden the indigenous part of their identity in the past, for fear of discrimination, but as the mood of the world has moved to be more in their favour, they may choose instead to emphasize it. In Canada and Australia, for example, Aboriginal arts are doing thriving business, and art is also an excellent way to demonstrate an element of continuity for their identity as a First Nation. In this case, the indigenous connection is being used in a way that the French anthropologist Pierre Bourdieu describes as *cultural capital*, a strategic use for a particular benefit. Researchers too need to be aware of history when they decide how to present their own identity. As mentioned in the introduction to this book, some Indigenous peoples resent anthropologists for their historical association with the past negative ranking of peoples and they are keen to do their own research, so it is important for new researchers to find a complementary role. In Bolivia, since an Indigenous president was elected, there is a political advantage to being a member of an indigenous group, and the government also employs anthropologists.

Language and other kinds of symbolism are also important elements in the construction of identity, and those who grow up bilingual, or multilingual, will be aware of different identities they can present in each language they use. Some will regularly switch between these different identities, and the sociolinguistic term *code-switching* refers to this kind of activity. Within one language, people may switch between different accents – for example using a local dialect at home, and a more standard form of the local language at school – and those who have the facility to adapt have another string to their bow of identity creation. Use of language, dress, and other forms of symbolism are good ways to express belonging, the subject of which we will consider in some detail in the next chapter. We will also return to the use of language as we consider how boundaries are created.

7

Ways of belonging

In this chapter, we will draw the threads of our discussions of personhood and ritual into a consideration of how the personal identity formed relates to the idea of belonging to a wider group. We will consider ways in which groups may be defined, and how boundaries are drawn around them. The symbolism of language, religion, and ethnicity will be examined in more detail here, showing how it is used to include and exclude, to discriminate and to dominate, and the effects that such divisions have on rights and access to resources. An important aspect of the discussion will be to examine the flexibility and flux of such boundaries, and the element of personal choice that may or may not exist in practice. The first section will consider some of the ways in which boundaries are drawn, the second, ways in which they are maintained, and the third will examine some of the different things that may be bounded.

Drawing boundaries

A preliminary way to draw boundaries around groups of people and their homes and possessions is to mark off the space in which they live, and there is considerable anthropological theory about this first method of defining groups. In chapter 6, we were introduced to Arnold van Gennep's rites of *territorial passage*, which express the basic principles of rites of passage in spatial terms, and his model of society as a house with rooms expresses well the need to mark, with ritual, the movement from one room to another. In practice, in some societies, people do actually mark a movement from one room of a house to another, as we shall see, but the principle operates at various other levels as well. Movement in and out of whole buildings is often marked, sometimes to identify *domestic space*, such as a home, but also to respect *sacred space*, such as a church, mosque, or temple. Entry into and out of a village or community may also be marked, and van Gennep offered some good examples, which usually also defined the kinds of territories that were taken as the focus of *political anthropology*. In today's world the most official form of boundary marking is indeed that set of border-crossing procedures that is designed to protect and defend *nations* from too much immigration. The subject of migration will be considered at great length in the next chapter, but the passage into – and out of – a *nation state*, especially if the journey is made by aeroplane, fits van Gennep's model rather well, although his book was written before air travel was much more than a dream. Unless one arrives with the appropriate documents, usually a passport and possibly a visa, it is in fact impossible to pass this boundary at all. There are official and social rituals to undertake even before leaving one's own land, including farewells to the family and passage through a security system, and then there is invariably a period of transition in a place which boasts goods available tax-free to mark its non-aligned status, and which has a definite feel of being in a liminal situation. On arrival at the new country, there is again the ritual of showing your documents and a passage through the customs area to assure the local authorities that illegal goods are not being imported. Those lucky enough to have family or friends to meet them will again engage in greetings, perhaps an exchange of gifts, and possibly a meal to celebrate the reunion and realignment of belonging.

Van Gennep's illustrations involved parallel rites passing into and out of a village, and some of these older customs may still be experienced in cultural parks and museums, if not so often in the countryside these days. For example, in Aotearoa or Māori

Figure 7.1 A Māori formal greeting challenges visitors before entrance to their marae, or meeting place.
© imagebroker / Alamy

New Zealand, there may be a challenge to outsiders arriving to visit a culture centre, or *marae*, and each party must check out the other in a ritualized fashion before they can proceed. Van Gennep also discusses the Jewish custom of touching a *mezuzah* before entering an orthodox house, and the dabbing of holy water to one's head on entering a Roman Catholic church. To enter a Japanese house, one must pause in a liminal zone known as a *genkan* to take off one's shoes, and there are special greetings which vary depending on whether one is coming in, or going out, and whether one is an insider or outsider to the

home – again reinforcing degrees of belonging. In this case, there is also a custom of donning slippers for certain parts of the house, but removing them on the rush matting that covers the most formal rooms, and a trip to the bathroom or toilet will require another change of footwear.

The space within a building may also be divided in order to separate groups of people according to important divisions within the society. In Pakistani homes, for example, some rooms are used by men and others by women; and although the women may enter the men's room to deliver food and drink, the men rarely penetrate the inner sanctum of the women. Such gendered divisions are quite common, as illustrated in an early collection of papers entitled *Women and Space*, edited by Shirley Ardener. A particularly detailed case of the Berber house, described and analysed by Pierre Bourdieu, has become a classic in this field, this time dividing insiders and guests as associated with lower and higher regions of the house respectively. This may be seen as parallel to the English expression 'upstairs and downstairs' that divides the family and visitors from the servants, and in large houses people might also designate spaces to separate the generations: a nursery for the children, and perhaps a special wing reserved for elderly members of the family.

These divisions are also found in special-purpose buildings such as kindergartens, schools, men's clubs, and old peoples' homes. In other societies, there may be a special hut for menstruating women, or a 'long-house' where men meet to discuss matters that anthropologists have described as *political*. In some rural Japanese communities, there used to be young peoples' inns, where those we call adolescents would stay during a period of transition between childhood and adulthood, offering a good opportunity for them to experiment with sexual relations and choose partners for their future family lives. Buildings associated with religious life are usually clearly divided from the profanity of secular life, and worshippers and visitors alike may be asked to

remove shoes, or cover their heads and shoulders. Sometimes, distinct areas are reserved for men and for women, and yet others for those who have been ordained into the special status of ministers or perhaps shamans, areas which are taboo to ordinary people.

At the level of neighbourhoods within towns and cities, there may be marked divisions between areas occupied by people of different origins, and those who stray into the 'wrong' zone will find themselves quite out of place. Belfast in Northern Ireland has a reputation as such a city, and New York City has developed similar elements, as has Montreal in Canada. The divisions in each of these cities are based on different principles, though. In Belfast, they reflect an unhappy divide between Protestant and Roman Catholic families, reinforced by the faith-based schools that many of the children attend, as well as the location of their churches. The division is more fundamentally based on differing political views, however, expressed forcibly each year when Protestants hold 'Orange' marches to celebrate the British seizure of land which many of the Roman Catholics still think should be part of an independent Ireland, and to which they therefore still express *resistance*. The division is thus also rooted in a *shared history* which each side passes down through the generations, but usually from the contrasting perspective of opponents in a series of bitter battles.

In New York, on the other hand, there are few original native inhabitants who seek to reclaim their former residence; instead the divisions are based on the ethnic and national associations of the people who have settled there over the years. Undoubtedly these originally reflected the desire of new arrivals to make homes near earlier settlers who shared their language and background, but eventually offering a mosaic of *ethnic difference* within the same city – Spanish Harlem, Little Italy, Irish Riviera, Chinatown, and so on. In Montreal, spatial divisions mark off areas occupied by different linguistic groups, predominantly

French and English, reflecting the historical divisions in the creation of Canada, but also including an area of Hebrew-speaking Orthodox Jews, and, just across the Lawrence river, a settlement of Mohawks who are working hard to revive a language which they lost for a couple of generations, when they were forced to submit to the assimilation policies of the Canadian government of the time. These three spatial city examples thus demonstrate several other major ways in which people define group membership, namely by language, ethnicity, and religion, all of which are backed up by an *ideology* of shared, though possibly contested, history.

In practice, in contemporary urban society, it is quite rare for group membership to be defined spatially, except for special occasions, although rural village societies will of course still maintain their territorial boundaries. Instead, people demonstrate their belonging by using symbolic markers (such as those we discussed in chapter 1 around the body, and in chapter 2 around other forms of communication). Male members of the orthodox Jewish community in Montreal, for example, as in many other places, grow their hair long, and wear distinctive black hats. In Jerusalem, orthodox Jewish women cover their arms, and many wear long skirts, thus making outsiders to their neighbourhoods immediately obvious, apparently an intentional part of trying to keep their neighbourhoods to themselves. In this same city, Christians and Muslims can also often be identified by their attire: Armenian priests wear tall black hats of a different shape to those worn by orthodox Jewish men, and Muslim women again wear long skirts, but also often wear veils. The use of the veil, *ḥijāb*, or the more all-enveloping *burqa* has introduced markers chosen by women around the world to express a religious or ethnic affiliation.

It is important to consider the element of choice when discussing how people use symbols to mark boundaries between themselves and others because outsiders to a group often make

Figure 7.2 Woman in burqa in Dubai.
© David Pearson / Alamy

erroneous assumptions, and these female garments offer a good case for consideration. For many Western observers the wearing of a ḥijāb or burqa represents female submission, but this is not the point at all, according to Fatima Mernissi. Indeed, Mernissi described the choice as *empowering*. It is actually quite informative to ask friends, and even strangers, why they wear particular identity markers – you may be surprised by their reasoning and decisions. The issue of choice also raises the question of flexibility, and Islamic clothes have been chosen by non-Muslim women journalists, perhaps to show respect, but also to enable safe travel through Islamic countries. They would be likely to wear quite different garments at home. Language, especially a local accent, is not so easy to hide, although some people become adept at *code-switching* for strategic reasons, perhaps to pass as a foreigner in an awkward situation – being stopped for speeding is one possibility, where the local police might be put off at the idea of having to speak a foreign tongue – or to persuade a potential client of one's impeccable upbringing! Scarification and permanent tattoos are also harder to hide, unless they are in intimate locations, but clothes are relatively easy to put on and take off according to the occasion.

Exclusion, discrimination, and domination

One good reason why people might want to hide their identity is because of the fear of *discrimination* by others in the wider society to which they belong. The practice of excluding, or discriminating against others is an often insidious, but very powerful means of maintaining groups, real or imaginary. Those who can be flexible, for example by choosing to wear different clothes or speak different languages, may be relatively protected against such treatment, but more obvious markers, such as the colour of one's skin or a strong foreign accent, are difficult to hide. Discrimination is often related to the exercise of *domination* within a complex society, and may thus also form part of the maintenance of a political system. However, there are long-standing social divisions based on institutions such as monarchy, to which we have already referred, which persist despite exercising very little in the way of power. In this section, we will consider some of the mechanisms used to maintain social groups, and a few of the consequences of powerful maintenance.

The most fierce and passionate examples of group definition arise in situations of *violence*, whether in full-scale war, enactments of local gang culture, or in situations regarded by one side as *terrorism*, by another as *resistance* or a bid for *freedom* from constraints considered unfair or even illegal. All social and cultural groups subscribe to systems of *value*, norms of behaviour often codified in *laws*, and even within those groups, those who fail to live up to the expectations of those systems may be subjected to violent *sanctions* such as arrest, punishment, or even execution. Ironically, perhaps, most sets of laws ostensibly prohibit murder and violence, but there are usually limits to the tolerance of the behaviour of others, and rationale such as retribution, self-defence, or protection of the innocent, are brought out to justify the taking of life. The study of these limits makes clear many of the ways in which boundaries are drawn, for it is when two or more systems of value come into direct or perceived conflict that the worst cases of violence may occur.

The names of particularly horrific examples, such as *ethnic genocide* or *ethnocide*, imply that the basis of the difference lies in distinctions of ethnicity, and anthropological research is particularly skilled at identifying the underlying causes for such violence. Usually historical factors are involved, such as stories passed down of previous ill treatment, sometimes many generations ago, but nevertheless horrific enough apparently to justify violent retribution. These may involve contested claims to land, and ritual celebration of its seizure by one side might trigger a reaction on the part of the other, as we saw for Northern Ireland. The building and break-up of the former Yugoslavia is another case in point. The country was created in the years following World War II, and for several decades held together several ethnic groups that also had a disputed history. Sadly, the union fell apart in 1990, and the strife that ensued was justified in terms of differences dating back to the fourteenth century. Durham anthropologist Iain Edgar has opened insights into the power of dreams to explain differences such as these, and he has also completed a study of the inspirational role of true dreams in the motivation of militant *jihad* by Al-Qaeda and Taliban leaders and followers.

The occupation of land has been a common cause for the destruction of whole peoples during periods of colonization, and justifications used at the time have been many and various, but usually expressing an idea of the superiority of the colonizing powers. When occupied peoples have fought back, they are described as terrorists, insurgents, or simply 'savage', as if an inequality in technological skill somehow justified the horror of eliminating them. Empire building has been an endeavour riddled with violence, at the very least for economic advantage, but more commonly to seize and claim territory, and to over-come and *dominate* local peoples.

Interestingly enough, many such peoples, though apparently fierce, had over millennia devised ingenious ways of resolving local conflict relatively peacefully, and several examples of *political anthropology* explain in detail these accommodations. An influen-tial example was the early-twentieth-century study conducted by E. E. Evans-Pritchard of the Nuer, now ironically one of the tribal peoples struggling to maintain their livelihoods in the war-torn situation of Southern Sudan. In the past, they did raid their neighbours, the Dinka, but neither side inflicted on the other anything like the kind of violence seen in that part of the world in recent times. Evans-Pritchard named the arrangements he observed as a *segmentary system*, and they exemplify a way of belonging that is quite recognizable, once identified and explained. Within the Nuer, the system was based on degrees of closeness to certain ancestors, all named, remembered, and sometimes recited as an expression of belonging and relatedness to people we would call siblings, cousins, and then simply more distant relatives.

In cases of dispute, Nuer people were accustomed to aligning themselves with their closest kin, back to the line of distinction between themselves and the other party in the dispute. *Feuds* would arise around such differences, sometimes perpetuated through several generations, and another aspect of the lives of the Nuer, namely that they regularly moved twice a year to find water sources for their cattle, allowed them to readjust their settlements and live with those they perceived as allies. Such accommodations sometimes deviated from the original kin connections, resulting in a system Evans-Pritchard also described as a case of fission / fusion politics. *Feuds* are a phenomenon found in many societies, and may lie dormant for years, but erupt into violence if members of the groups concerned cross unacceptable boundaries, such as falling in love with a member of the wrong group, as dramatized in fictional scenarios such as *Romeo and Juliet* and *West Side Story*.

Another way in which groups maintain their boundaries without resorting to unacceptable degrees of violence is by ritualizing their differences, and sport is a good contemporary example. The way in which people support teams playing their favourite sport is also another example of the segmentary system, as it happens, for the alignment varies depending on the degree of separation from the team heroes who are playing at any particular game. Thus, groups of supporters who line up against one another at a game in the local stadium may find themselves on the same side for a national encounter. Likewise, in school tournaments, those who support a particular school at one game may find themselves side by side with their 'enemies' at a county match, and again with those enemies at a national one. To assist with understanding the segmentary system, Evans-Pritchard gave the example of how one would answer the question 'where are you from?' depending on where you were being asked. Within a street, you would give the house number, within a town or city, the street name, in another location, the town name, and so forth. Only in a foreign land would you name your country of origin.

The building of nation states around the world has involved much attention to inculcating pride in belonging, and there are many examples to observe, typically using ritual events that evoke strong emotions in their participants. The 'Orange' marches in Northern Ireland were mentioned above, and these are but one example of occasions when people don uniforms, bang drums, play stirring music, and strut about to express allegiance to their kind and their country. Appropriate symbolism is chosen to express the particular nation: a flag and its colours, a national anthem, some typical garments, a local flower, bird, or animal, and perhaps some invention or technological achievement of which the nation is particularly proud. Military marches may parade tanks, guns, and other weapons of power, and haunting music will accompany laments for the soldiers who have fallen in the face of such machinery. On sporting occasions, such as the Olympic Games, or the Soccer World Cup, the competition is still passionate, but ritually contained so that supporters who express violence are deemed to be 'hooligans' and subject to strong disapproval and strict local sanctions.

In Britain, some of the most elaborate boundary-marking ritual are those associated with the monarchy, and the announce-ment of the Royal Wedding of Prince William and Catherine Middleton in 2011 was widely deemed to be unmitigated good news, despite falling in a period of severe economic depression. Tourists visiting London for the first time inevitably make their way to see daily events such as the Changing of the Guard at Buckingham Palace, when the paths of marching soldiers are firmly confined, and their garments much more for show than for any acts of physical defence, or to the Tower of London, a site of horrific punishments in the past, but now just another location of elaborate cultural display. Rituals of royalty are not found in every nation, and even where they are found, some 'subjects' will be resentful about their cost, but they are powerful expressions of social groupings that can evoke the strongest expressions of loyalty, especially where the incumbents of the primary roles somehow express ideological expectations popular with their people at the time. Public reaction to the death of Princess Diana was an example of loyalty so powerful that it surprised even some of the anthropologists who specialize in these issues.

At this point, it is useful to return to the element of choice that is thought to characterize many complex societies, even to be a *sine qua non* of civilized life, among those devising political policies and seeking the support of their potential voters. It can clearly be linked to the idea, raised in chapter 5, of the 'cult of the individual', since subscribing to an idea of one's own choice and allegiance has a powerful appeal. An individual member of society may choose to be loyal to a monarchy, or to reject it, and today that person would not expect that he or she would go to war over issues that underpinned many a bloody civil war in Europe over the centuries. The defence of this kind of freedom is one of the things that evokes strong emotions, however, and when it is expressed as underpinning *democracy*, it can sometimes be powerful enough to drive a people to invade the lands of those who fail to recognize the concept's value. Ideals of *human rights*, enshrined by international bodies such as the United Nations, may be called upon to justify considerable violence in the face of perceived exploitation, but anthropology as a discipline warns us to be careful not to impose our own upbringing and values on others.

Thus, a friendly expression of the Irish presence in New York is the celebration of St Patrick's Day, when green beer is served and people from all sorts of backgrounds dress as leprechauns and other characters of Irish origin. On the other hand, since the 9/11 attack on the World Trade Center, which killed and maimed a large number of New Yorkers, as well as temporary residents from various other countries, a much less friendly division has arisen, pitting New Yorkers from a range of backgrounds against fellow citizens who happen to share the same religious allegiance as the attackers. This mistaken conflation of the religious association of the *fundamentalists* who committed the crime with that of ordinary people who have nothing else in common with them, political, historical, or ideological, illustrates very neatly the power of violence to engender feelings of discrimination. The situation also offers an example of the limits, in one specific case, of laws and ideals against murder and violence, for non-violence is one of the principles of Islam, and a study of the reasons for the *jihad* that underpins the behaviour of those deemed by Americans to be terrorists might help to resolve some of the issues.

Human, animal, spirit, or cyborg

In chapter 1, we briefly mentioned an article by Edmund Leach, who argued that humans use language – in English, anyway – to distinguish themselves from animals, especially those that provide food or live in close proximity with them, by using versions of their names in terms of abuse. Cows, pigs, sheep, dogs, cats, and chickens may all have their names taken in this way so that to describe a person as an animal – 'you pig' or 'that was catty' – is usually an unwanted and therefore negative thing to do. On the other hand, some specific animals may be regarded as members of human groups – pets like cats and dogs are seen as part of the family, for example – so this boundary-marking between animals and humans becomes blurred. In other societies and languages, there are many other examples, and diverse languages classify different animals in alternative ways, as mentioned in the case of animals used as the name of a clan. Members of the same clan share group membership based on their relationship with the bird or animal of their clan.

Relationships with special animals such as these are also very varied, usually described in stories handed down through the generations, or read to children as they are growing up.

One popular theme is that an animal can become a helpmate in times of difficulty, and a particular person may associate with a very specific animal, sometimes known as a familiar. Another theme is the idea of transformation between human and animal form, so breaking down completely any strict separation between the worlds of humans and other animals. The American coyote is a common character in Native American *trickster* stories, for example, where he can turn himself into a human to perform his tricks. In European stories, a prince may appear disguised as a frog, an ogre may convert himself into a mouse, or a man may become a werewolf at the time of a full moon. In Latin American ethnography, there are several examples of shamans who are said to be capable of transforming themselves into an animal such as a jaguar, perhaps in order to travel to another world to fulfil some request from a client.

This case is an example of an animal providing a bridge with a spiritual world; another is found in Japan, where cats in a shrine may be thought of as messengers from the gods. Spirits appearing in animal form may also be believed to be humans returning from the world of the afterlife to visit a living relative, and there is another set of ethnography about the ways in which humans may be transformed into spirits in order to make such a transition during their lives. Dreams are commonly interpreted as a chance to meet those who have 'passed on', to experience warnings or advice from a member of another world, or to travel to another world oneself. In many societies, humans and other living beings are thought to have a soul or spirit that can travel independently of the body, and that lives on after the body dies. Reference is made in their lives to the existence of this soul and the role it might play in the future world of the living. Again, some specialists – sometimes called spirit mediums – are said to be adept at enabling such communication, and interviewing such a specialist would be an excellent way for an anthropologist to gain access to the shared ideas of a particular group.

A contemporary form of human transformation that has formed the focus of high-tech storytelling, like films and video games, is the idea of a 'scientifically' modified human being such as a cyborg, or more recently an *avatar*, the latter picking up a word previously used to describe a human manifestation of the Hindu god Vishnu. The film *Avatar* is one example of the modern use of this word, and raises issues with parallels in relations between human worlds that will be discussed in the next chapter, but video games have for some time offered players the chance to create their own avatar, or *second life*, that lives in a virtual world of their own making. A recent anthropological interest has been in the way that people design and practice relationships in such a world.

Cyborgs have also intrigued scholars. These are beings whose original human bodies have been more or less mechanized, from a small but vital transformation like a heart pacemaker or a hearing aid, to a complete makeover forming a *bionic* man or woman of the sort that appears, in science fiction stories and films. The word comes from the concept of *cybernetic organisms*, and the interest of scholars has been in how these transformations might change the identity of the original person, among other things. They remain different from robots in that the starting point of a cyborg is a human body, whereas a robot starts out as a machine and may or may not be designed to look like a human, although some science fiction robots have been presented with very human characteristics that may or may not appear in the future, and boundaries between them may become blurred. A cloned human being is another potentially interesting phenomenon, as are the social and cultural dimensions of *organ transplants* and *artificial limbs* that have formed the focus of an intriguing anthropological study by Margaret Lock.

Ethical issues have formed the focus of much of the research to date on the social effects of increasingly clever *medical technologies*, or more general *biotechnology*. The striving among humans to *make* humans is regarded as unethical by many, especially for those who feel that this should remain the domain of a god or gods. It follows that attempts to make animals have also triggered a significant backlash, usually amongst those humans who feel that these animals are being treated cruelly, or simply shouldn't be created for experiments in the first place. The conflict between the interests of humans and the interests of other animals is explored in a number of cases in the collection *Natural Enemies,* edited by John Knight.

8

The global species

This and the next chapter of the book will bring the materials we have studied about people in different societies into a global context. The first approach we will take dates back, through archaeological and fossil research, to the earliest examples of human dispersal. We will begin by laying out more detailed theories of human origins, in particular ecological and genetic explanations of biological and social differences between various human populations, and how they came to settle in widely separated areas of the world.

We will then turn to the resources social and cultural anthropologists have used to discuss migration and settlement patterns as well as the dissemination of cultural forms, such as music and food. We will consider theories surrounding the process that has become known as *globalization*, a term whose use basically coincides with the extraordinary increase in the speed of the spread of people and ideas in the past few decades. There are many disciplines that have addressed issues of globalization and, more recently, the internet, but anthropology and in-depth ethnographic study bring particular value to understanding their *local* effects.

The origins of a globalized species

Although today we take it for granted that humans inhabit almost every corner of the planet our status as a global species is a relatively recent phenomenon. We can all trace our ancestry back to the same region of Africa, the Omo Valley in Ethiopia. It is here that we find the oldest example of the skeleton of *Homo sapiens* and it is also where genetic analysis suggests we originate – the so-called Out of Africa model. The pattern of human global dispersal is one that closely reflects the pattern of our evolutionary development over the last two hundred thousand years. It is often incorrectly thought that we are the only human species and that we have always lived in a world empty of other human species. Yet when *Homo sapiens* started to expand out of Africa it was not the only species of human that inhabited the world. In Europe, there were the Neanderthals, in Asia *Homo erectus* and *Homo floresiensis* while in the Altai Mountains of Siberia we would have found 'Species X' or the Denisova hominin which is unique in being based purely on genetic identification rather than anatomical description.

When we dispersed beyond Africa remains a subject of debate in palaeoanthropology but by at least one hundred thousand years ago we start to find fossils of *Homo sapiens* outside of Africa for the first time. The earliest examples are found around Mount Carmel in Israel and date to around ninety thousand years ago. We can then start to see a push eastwards with *Homo sapiens* appearing in Asia by about seventy thousand years ago and Australia perhaps as early as sixty thousand years ago (sea levels were much lower and modern day Australia would have been part of the same land mass as the New Guinean land mass). Humans didn't reach Europe until around forty thousand years ago and recent genetic research, conducted by Svante Pääbo at the Max Planck Institute for Evolutionary Anthropology in Germany, seems to suggest that *Homo sapiens* came into contact with Neanderthals in Europe and that some limited interbreeding, or gene flow, may have taken place between the two species. According to Pääbo, between one percent and four percent of the genome in people of Eurasian descent comes from genetic mixing with Neanderthals. (This poses a small spanner in the works for the Out of Africa theory, which – if the data holds up – will need to be modified to accommodate this gene flow.) But the widespread dispersal of *Homo sapiens* beyond its traditional home of East Africa seems to have sounded the death knell for other members of the genus *Homo*. By 50,000 years ago all trace of *Homo erectus* in Asia has disappeared, by 28,000 years ago the Neanderthals disappear from their last European refuge on the Iberian Peninsula and by approximately thirteen thousand years ago the intriguing 'hobbit' *Homo floresiensis* is no longer found on the island of Flores (although ongoing excavations may alter this date in the coming years).

As other humans dwindled, *Homo sapiens* completed its domination of the planet. In several waves of migration, they reached the Americas – though anthropologists and Indigenous scholars debate exactly how and exactly when. During the glacial period, from approximately thirty thousand to twenty thousand years ago, ice covered the Bering Strait separating Asia and North America and a land bridge, called Beringia, linked the two continents, which would have allowed humans to continue their settlement eastwards. By eleven thousand years ago, humans were living at the southern tip of South America. Extremely isolated areas, such as Easter Island in the Pacific Ocean, were not inhabited until around one thousand years ago.

Much debate has surrounded how modern humans evolved (i.e., the advent of *Homo sapiens,* or anatomically modern humans). There are three main models that have been developed to explain the pattern and processes we can see in the fossil, genetic, and archaeological records: Out of Africa, Multiregional Continuity, and Assimilation.

THREE MODELS OF HUMANS ON THE MOVE

Coming out of the debate that has surrounded the origins and evolution of *Homo sapiens*, biological anthropologists have developed three major models that seek to explain the pattern and processes that are visible in fossil, genetic, and archaeological records:

- **Out of Africa**: The suite of modern behaviours, culture, and biology of *Homo sapiens* evolved in Africa around two hundred thousand years ago; When *Homo sapiens* began to disperse beyond Africa from around one hundred thousand years ago and moved across the Old World, replacing all of the other pre-existing hominin populations with little or no interbreeding.
- **Multiregional continuity**: *Homo sapiens* evolved from earlier hominin species that had previously left Africa, such as *Homo erectus* in Asia and *Homo heidelbergensis* in Europe, with significant gene flow between populations on the fringes of each region as well as adaptations to different environmental conditions. The differences between modern human populations today would be the result of the retention of some traits found in the original hominin inhabitants of each area.
- **Assimilation**: *Homo sapiens* evolved first in Africa before dispersing around the globe and exchanging some genes with other human species already present in Europe and Asia.

At the current time, almost all of the data that we have found supports the 'Out of Africa' model, although recent work that suggests some interbreeding with the Neanderthals may have taken place means that a modified form of 'Out of Africa' that allows for greater elements of gene-flow may well have to be considered. The paths taken may have differed but the story was the same: humans arrived and began to shape their new lands. First, as hunters and gatherers or pastoralists, but later as farmers who often cleared forests for agriculture and grazing, creating the landscapes with which we are familiar today.

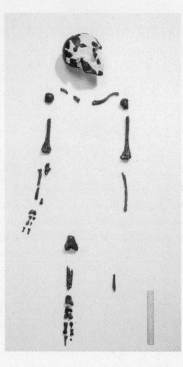

Figure 8.1 The earliest known fossil of *Homo sapiens*, around 200,000 years old. The bones and skull were found in 1967 by Richard Leakey and his team digging in Kibish, Ethiopa, east of the River Omo.

Fossil evidence is not the only data we can use to reconstruct the pattern of modern human movements. Broadly, the same pattern can be found in the genetic evidence for modern human evolution. Analysis of mitochondrial DNA (mtDNA), the DNA contained in a cell's mitochondria, which supplies it with the energy necessary to work, provides an intriguing picture of human movement. In humans, mitochondrial DNA is inherited from the mother, so it allows us to see how genes have been inherited through a line of mothers, all the way back to the so-called mitochondrial Eve, the common female ancestor of all *Homo sapiens*. This analysis points towards a shared African origin at around two hundred thousand years ago. And a similar pattern can be seen in data from the Y chromosome, the sex chromosome that makes a person male rather than female. (People normally carry two sex chromosomes: men are XY and women are XX.) If we combine the fossil and genetic information we get a very clear picture.

Humans appear first in Africa with modern behaviours and technologies before moving out of Africa and replacing the in situ species of *Homo* with little or no genetic mixing. If we consider the impact that the arrival of humans had on large mammals such as the American Mammoth, it is perhaps not going too far to suggest that we may also have had a bloody hand in the disappearance of our cousins. The mammoth – a massive animal, nearly four metres high and weighing around eight tonnes – roamed across North America and had survived several warming periods in the Earth's geological history. Yet shortly after *Homo sapiens* arrived in the Americas, the species was wiped out.

Modern diversity yet one ancestor

The evidence from biological anthropology presents us with a question. If all humans have such a recent common ancestor, and all originate from the same place, how do anthropologists explain the differences between humans that are clearly visible today? The human body exhibits a huge range of skin colours, and numerous languages are spoken around the world. If we all come from one original ancestral population based in the Omo Valley some two hundred thousand years ago, why don't we all look the same and understand each other's languages – let alone ways of life? If we examine the diversity that exists within the human species, we can perhaps identify two main factors in the creation of diversity: environment and sexual selection.

As we saw in chapter 4, environmental conditions can exert a huge influence on the human body, or phenotype, a force that is more than capable of suppressing or reducing the influence of our genes. Take the simple example of skin colour, which was touched upon earlier. Dark skin is more frequent in hot, equatorial environments, while light skin is more common in colder, northern latitudes. Here there is a clear biological relationship between the concentration of melanin (the pigment cells in the skin), exposure to sunlight, and synthesis of vitamin D, which is critical to the development of strong, healthy bones. When a person's skin is exposed to sunlight, the ultra-violet radiation naturally triggers the production of vitamin D, but prolonged UV exposure can also cause severe burning. Near the equator, the skin needed to be protected from too much radiation, and melanin helped to block this radiation, serving as a natural sun cream. As our ancestors moved north, they were exposed to less sunlight, and in turn less melanin was required to protect the skin from burning and more UV radiation was required to synthesize vitamin D – so less melanin and lighter skin. Today, we can use manufactured sun creams and take vitamin D supplements, but for most of human evolutionary history, melanin levels in the skin had to adapt to the environment, leading to the variation we see in our species today. A somewhat similar effect can be identified in the general regional patterns of body size and shape. Populations of humans living in hot environments tended to develop tall and lean bodies, which allowed large amounts of heat to be diverted away from the core along the limbs without the insulation of fat; populations living in arctic environments tended towards shorter and squatter bodies, better suited for conserving heat.

Sexual selection may also be a powerful force in creating the variation of humans from region to region. Specific attributes

that are attractive to the opposite sex can become rapidly established within a population, whether for purely biological reasons
or through a combination of biology and culture. Charles Darwin,
in his book *On the Origin of Species,* mentioned one of the most
well-known examples of sexual selection: the ornate peacock's
tail. Though it is quite large, the amazing beauty of the peacock's
tail attracts female partners, most likely because it shows how
healthy an individual is compared to his rivals. We can see a
number of analogous *dimorphic* traits in humans, where men
and women have different anatomical features, which may be
artefacts of sexual selection in our evolutionary past. These
include prominent female breasts (human female breasts are
much larger than those of other primates) and male facial hair (an
exception to the relative hairlessness of humans compared
to other primates). Some have argued that in relatively isolated
populations the effect of sexual selection can become much more
focused, with sexual attraction altering the distribution of a small
number of genes and leading to the prevalence of particular
physical traits.

As is often the case in human evolution, no pattern is, alas,
that simple. A human being may be the only animal that is utterly
dependent upon culture for its survival, but we also use culture
to entertain, to express ourselves, and to ornament our bodies.
Any biological appearances must also take into account the role
played by cultural adaptation; we are more than the sum of our
genes. For instance, skin colour is often lighter in the Middle East
than at parallel latitudes in Africa. To what extent could
skin colour have been affected by forms of dress in the region,
which have traditionally covered the body, keeping it cool and
protecting it from the sun? Perhaps this cultural adaptation
removed some of the need for the body to produce more
melanin in the skin. There is also the complication that the
Middle East stands at the crossroads of several continents, and
for the past couple of thousand years has been an important

trade route. Perhaps economic exchanges went hand in hand with marriages, changing skin colour through regional gene flow. Likewise, the skin colour found among many groups living in the Arctic is not as pale as you might expect, given the high north latitude of their habitat. Partly, this may be a result of the high-protein diet common in these areas, where vegetation is scarce and people tend to consume a large amount of fish and other meats – with fatty fish providing a particularly good source of vitamin D. So though these same groups must wear clothing to protect them from the extreme cold, the reduced sunlight exposure has less of an effect on skin colour. These cultural adap-tations solved multiple biological problems posed by living in such an environment. Thus, although a number of genes have been associated with different skin tones, particularly clustered around regional populations, the variation evident in humans living today comes out of a combination of sex, environment, and culture – it's far more complex than genetics.

Disease patterns also provide an intriguing source of data for understanding human evolution and variation. One classic example adorns many a biology textbook: the distribution of sickle cell anaemia. Although three quarters of sickle cell disease cases are found in Africa, it is not an African disease, and it is not restricted to any one skin colour. Sickle cell anaemia occurs when a person carries two copies of the recessive gene for the disease, one inherited from the mother and the other from the father – what is called an autosomal recessive disorder. (Having only one gene makes you a carrier – someone who does not have the disease itself but can pass it on to a child.) When the two genes are activated, or expressed, they alter the shape of the blood cells in the body, morphing them from the pliable, donut-like norm to the rigid hook of a sickle. This change obstructs the blood's natural flow through the body and can lead to organ damage, severely reducing a person's life expectancy. Why would evolution develop this genetic trait, let alone allow it to survive, generation after generation?

As it happens, the sickle cell gene does benefit humans: a person who has only one copy of the recessive gene will usually produce a few sickled cells in their bloodstream. These will not pose a threat to the carrier's health; however, these few cells provide a high degree of protection against the even more threatening tropical disease, malaria. The most lethal form of malaria in humans involves the parasite *Plasmodium falciparum*, which infects red blood cells and leads to fever, shivering, vomiting, headache, and sometimes coma or death. *Plasmodium falciparum*, however, cannot infect the sickled cells – there's not enough oxygen in them for the parasite to reproduce. So having some sickled blood cells gives you an evolutionary advantage in an environment where you might contract malaria. The global distribution of sickle cell disease maps almost precisely the historical distribution of the species of mosquito that serves as a carrier for the *Plasmodium* parasite while it's waiting to find its next human body host: Sub-Saharan Africa, Asia, North and South America, the Mediterranean (and now, associated disasporic populations). This neat evolutionary adaptation shows how genetic variations between humans can result from environmental pressures.

As scientists in the early part of the twentieth century began to unravel how malaria is spread, they realized that they did not have to attack the *Plasmodium* parasite with a vaccine, and they did not have to find some way to morph normal blood cells into sickled ones: they simply had to decrease the number of mosquitoes, so that the parasite had fewer places to call home when it was not in a human. Marshes and other wetlands were often drained, thus destroying the malaria-carrying mosquito's nearby habitats (and providing extra land for farming). More recently, mosquito nets have been distributed throughout malaria-prone regions, at the cost of a few pennies each. These are cultural solutions to a biological problem, but, as we have seen, natural selection does not work on short timelines – it works across the long history of evolution, over tens of thousands of years. For this reason, sickle cell disease still exists, even though humans now have other safer ways to prevent malaria.

The story of sickle cell anaemia helps to explain why many diseases that appear on the face of it to have no evolutionary advantage to humans exist. For example, why do humans get cancer? Why haven't the genes associated with cancer been 'selected against' for the fitness of the species? Taking the view of our evolutionary past, the fact is that most cancers do not appear until an age at which most of our human ancestors would already have been long dead; life expectancy was much shorter for most of human history, not just in evolutionary terms. Most cancers also appear well after the prime reproductive period of life, meaning that they would have little effect on whether a particular individual was able to pass on his or her genes to children. It is more accurate, then, to think of these genes as 'selectively neutral', because they do not impact on the ability to reproduce. No sexual selection is involved.

Similarly, the long view of evolution explains many curiosities of modern human anatomy, including wisdom teeth (the third set of molars, which do not appear until the late teens) and seemingly needless organs like the appendix. Close to thirty-five percent of people today never develop wisdom teeth, and many who do experience pain and discomfort from them. Why do we have them at all? The theory is that early humans needed these heavy-duty molars to chew plants, which then made up the bulk of their diet. Likewise, the appendix seems to be all that remains of the cecum, a digestive organ that hosts bacteria that can digest the tough cellulose in plants; many herbivores today have one. As humans invented fire and ate cooked (i.e., softer) plants and meats, the jaw became smaller (leaving little room for wisdom teeth), and the cecum shrunk, but the teeth and appendix have not yet been written out of our biological code. To our modern eyes, these anatomical features – which are called vestigial structures, since they are surviving traces of the past – seem pointless in light of the cultural adaptation of cooking. But there is also little pressure for these features to be selected against, especially now that doctors can treat appendicitis and problematic wisdom teeth.

In this way, cultural development has shaped our biological evolution, because humans generally use culture to circumvent the problems that any other organism must fall back on biological adaptation to solve. This has allowed us to populate the entire planet, while most other species have a limited range – sometimes so limited that we may not even know that we've destroyed their habitat, and perhaps the entire species, by ploughing through a quarter acre of rainforest.

There are, however, trade-offs to being as skilled at adaptation and migration as humans are. As we've travelled the globe, we've become hosts for bacteria and viruses that evolve faster than we do. And even though we can now use antibiotics to treat infections, the bacteria are increasingly resistant to our inventions. Just as we come up with a cultural trick to defeat one strain, another evolves that is immune. After all, evolution is not just something that happens to humans!

Historical and cultural evidence of migration

Social and cultural anthropologists also collect evidence of the movement of peoples and their cultural creations, and our studies of specific peoples usually start out with an attempt to place them within their own geographical and historical context. The sources of evidence depend very much on the local situation. Literate peoples have their own written records which may or may not have been translated into outside languages, so anthropologists might benefit from co-operation with local historians; non-literate peoples will also have a rich fund of stories about their own origins, and these comprise *oral history*, along with information they provide about neighbouring peoples and the relations between them. Just as with historical records, orally transmitted stories present situations from different points of view, so that the perspective of the neighbours themselves may be quite a contrast. The way that such stories are used in contemporary situations is a subject that anthropologists are well qualified to assess; if we have a deep understanding of the specific peoples, so we have a helpful role to play when migrations lead to conflict.

Another major source of evidence of the movement of peoples is to be found in their *material culture*, which is also studied in the field of archaeology. *Ethnographic museums* around the world have gathered collections from a wide range of geographical locations, enabling assessments to be made about the degree to which peoples have influenced one another, or traded the goods they produce by carrying them to distant markets. The layout of the Pitt Rivers Museum in Oxford is designed to allow objects with similar practical applications but different origins to be compared, and this reflects the *diffusionist* theoretical ideas of Lieutenant-General Augustus Henry Lane-Fox Pitt Rivers who started the collections. He gave them to Oxford University on the understanding that the curators maintain this form of display.

A more recent, but in some ways parallel approach, has been developed by the Indian anthropologist Arjun Appadurai, based at New York University, who examines what he calls 'the social life of things', referring to the variety of value and meaning the same objects may acquire in different cultural settings. Thus, an object which in the location where it was constructed served a practical function, say for carrying goods, or serving food, may in another become an object of exotic art, or even a means of currency. This approach opened up a new way of interpreting the movement of material culture, particularly in a world where things are moving around fast enough to be followed by the same individual observer. A further focus on the saleable value that may become attached to an object as it moves around is known as *commodification*, a term used in the study of economics. An accessible study which adds an anthropological dimension – the social and cultural aspects – is a book entitled *The World of Goods*, edited by Mary Douglas and Baron Isherwood.

The third set of evidence of the migration of people we can collect as anthropologists is of less tangible cultural items, such as dance and music, and we have specialist *ethnomusicologists* who focus on these aspects of human creativity. Their studies are, of course, aided by the collection of instruments that people took with them as they travelled, but they also make studies of the influence of musical forms and styles of movement. In recent times, there is almost no time lag in the transmission of musical forms, and a whole new phenomenon known as *world music* offers a cornucopia of music and dance to anyone with a computer or a television set. There are, of course, people who try to identify the different sources of the styles and rhythms, but the phenomenon of world music has taken on a cultural form of its own, characteristic of our new *globalized* world.

Markets, colonialism, and 'development'

Theories about aspects of what has become known as *globalization* have been made by scholars in many disciplines, but another area in which anthropologists have made a special contribution is in looking at the movement of food, drink, and the plants to produce them. Examining the way that food has been adopted and adapted to local situations opens up an intimate understanding of issues that lie at the heart of capitalism and colonialism. As we have seen, these studies link our bodies, our language, our social relations, and our environment. On the ground in specific locations, food and drink from another part of the world takes on a value of its own again, just as do the objects of material culture.

Sometimes this value has become so important to the people who produce, market and/or consume such nutrients that they become a prime source of local identity, a source so strong that it may combine elements of healing with a reason to go to war!

Consider, for example, the value accorded by people in different countries around the world to an apparently simple cup of tea. Many people in England drink several cups or mugs of tea every day of their adult lives; they will collect a variety of 'herbal teas' for particular occasions, or they will prefer 'ordinary' black tea, with or without milk and that other global product: sugar. People in England offer cups of tea to cheer those who are feeling low, they produce strong and sweetened tea for victims of an accident or a shock, and they arrange their best crockery to serve it to their most respected guests. Tea is the one substance that is readily available in everyone's kitchen, yet it has never been a local product, and it must always be imported from abroad, as must the sugar that sweetens it.

Tea does grow in India, China, and Japan, and it is consumed avidly in each of these countries as well, but it is prepared and served differently in each place. In India, a popular brew of black (roasted) tea will be presented with plenty of milk and mixed with a selection of spices and herbs, in China, the relatively unprocessed green tea leaves are simply doused with hot water, possibly several times over. In Japan, a powdered green tea known as *macha* is prepared in a highly formalized ceremony, which has been refined to incorporate ideas about the surroundings for its consumption, the clothes that must be worn for the occasion, the style of seating during the process, and the very words which are, or mostly are not, to be spoken while the tea is offered. The cups which are used may be works of art worth a small fortune, yet the same word for a tea cup, *chawan*, is also used for the mundane holder of the daily bowls of rice.

All these aspects of tea culture, and of many other foods and drinks, have been studied by anthropologists. A classic book about sugar by American anthropologist Sidney Mintz, called *Sweetness and Power*, puts the production and consumption of sugar around the world in the context of global markets and colonization. As sugary tea became the preferred beverage of almost everyone in Britain, a major task of imperial expansion was to secure economically viable sources for its constituents, and British relations with the Chinese soured considerably after the failure of Lord Macartney's mission to reach trade agreements with the Emperor Qianlong in 1793. British settlers in colonies with appropriate climates built huge tea and sugar plantations, and if the local people weren't willing or able to assist with the work, slaves were shipped in from Africa, and later, paid workers brought in from countries such as India, where the British had already established a strong imperial presence.

Figure 8.2 Kaeko Chiba, author of an anthropological thesis about tea in Japan conducts a ceremony in Boston, Massachusetts, home of a famous dispute about tea, as it made its way around the world. Photograph by Dhammadipa Sak

As well as gathering goods from around the world to bring back to their home countries, colonizing nations also exported a large measure of their own culture. Immediately in the wake of the traders would follow missionaries determined to 'save the poor infidels who had yet to hear of the true way'. The tracking of religious ideas, and observations about how imported faiths adapted prior ideas, or even built on existing beliefs and practice, has been another interest of anthropologists, which dates back to early history, and persists to the present day. Traders, missionaries, and the colonial administrators who seized local power would all import elements of their own culture, and more often than not, they destroyed much of the culture of the people whose lives they changed forever. Such arrogance has been justified again and again by dominant peoples who claim that they are bringing the benefits of their superior lives to the peoples they crush, and anthropologists have themselves sometimes been complicit in recent European incursions into foreign lands.

One legacy of this last bout of colonialism is couched in a rather insidious vocabulary of *progress* and *development*, which perpetuates the idea of superiority of the peoples who introduced advanced technology around the world. Taken together with the economic power that the technology has enabled, for example to extract wealth from the earth and to build weapons, it has been relatively easy for a limited number of nations to dominate the whole global system. Some of these nations have built up a shared set of values, which they perceive to be 'advanced': for example, political arrangements should be democratic; all peoples everywhere should observe what they have deemed to be basic human rights; and economic activity should be underpinned by the system known as *capitalism*.

For peoples who have yet to achieve what these nations define as *progress*, the rich of this global world have engaged in providing support for what they describe as *development*, and again anthropologists have sometimes been practically involved in administering support to areas where they have worked. This is a large-scale example of the principles of exchange and reciprocity that we discussed in chapter 3, but remember that those who have more wealth acquire more status. It may seem to be fair that those who extract wealth from the land that they have taken should invest in the welfare of the people who originally lived there, but often too little is done to learn about and value the long-term knowledge that those inhabitants have built up, or to take enough account of their perspective on a situation. The anthropology of development examines such issues, with special attention to the amount that can be learned from these oppressed peoples.

The backlash against globalization

One of the curious consequences of the phenomenon of globalization is a kind of backlash against the threat of homogenization which some social scientists predicted. As American and European goods spread rapidly around the world these theorists imagined that Euro-American ways of doing things would follow in their wake, and that cultural differences would fade away. This theory reflects the idea that industrial *development* brought with it a *modern*, rational way of thinking that would replace the different thought processes that they associated with the pre-modern, and its various versions became known as *theories of modernity*. To explain difficulties when their original predictions failed to be achieved, another set of theories known as *post-modern* followed them.

A first consequence of these ideas was that people who continued to express cultural difference became *marginalized* in one way or another, and disciplines such as economics and political science, which seek to derive broad predictions based on the principles of modernity, struggled to incorporate such variety into their theories. For a period, anthropology, too, became a marginalized discipline alongside these big players, and the idea of cultural explanation was – and sometimes still is – belittled by them. A few sociologists also seek to build big theories that will override cultural difference, and respond to a need perceived by disciplines that rely heavily on statistics and other *quantitative* indicators to be able to predict and replicate ideas within any social context. Others have become aware of the value of *qualitative* research, especially to understand local variety, and these are likely to work more closely with anthropologists in any particular context.

An example of the expression of marginality of people who continue to express cultural difference, which reflected the ease and speed of travel that came with globalization, was the sudden rise of theme parks and cultural centres that chose culture as a theme to display to visitors. A book by the anthropologist and art historian Nick Stanley entitled *Being Ourselves for You* includes examples from all over the world of parks, museums, and play-grounds that use cultural variety to attract their visitors. He also summarizes various theories about whether and why these parks marginalize the people on display, and an important factor is, of course, whether the people are doing their own displays or being displayed by others, and if the former, how representative the parks seem to other members of the groups on display.

The backlash referred to at the start of this section has been recognized more recently, but it relates precisely to this distinction, because there is also presently in place a widespread revival of cultural difference expressed by those who reject ideas of Americanization, homogenization, or even *nationalism* in favour of their own tried and tested ways of doing things. Within the European community, for example, many ethnic groups previously marginalized by the state into which they have been incorporated, are gaining more and more recognition of their own languages, identity, and rituals, so visitors to Spain will soon find themselves to be within Catalonia, Andalusia, or Galicia as well. In some cases, bigger nations are dividing up into smaller ones, with more or less violence, and the breakup of the Soviet Union is a prime example; others include the former states of Yugoslavia and Czechoslovakia.

A third example is the movement of revival of those Indigenous peoples who have formed standing committees at the United Nations – a topic we will consider in more detail in the next chapter.

9

Anthropology in the age of global communication

The *migration* of peoples is an old phenomenon which can be traced back in various ways to build up a global pattern of the movement of ideas and objects as well as the people who carried them. In this chapter, the focus will move right to the heart of the communities where migration is taking place. It will examine some of the reasons for out-migration, look at the ways people settle – or otherwise – in their new locations, and consider how earlier inhabitants react to their incoming neighbours. A popular subject of study is the extent to which the people who are moving keep in touch with relatives they have left behind, whether they send back resources and plan eventually to return, or whether they try instead to integrate themselves and their families into the new environment. Questions considered earlier – about kinship, personhood, and identity – are relevant to consider again in this new context, and scholars of migration often choose one or more of them as a focus.

Why people move

While migration today reflects our increased access to knowledge, the desire to move is as ancient as humans themselves. Many people attempt to move around the world for economic reasons,

often simply to take advantage of the possibilities another location seems to offer for improving their quality of life. In some
cases, where the migrant has skills to offer, or is willing to take
work that local people dislike, the situation can be mutually beneficial, an example of *reciprocity* where each side receives some
gain in the transaction. In other cases, or with the passage of time,
such movement can cause immense conflict at a local level, particularly in a time of high unemployment.

The settler communities of countries such as Australia,
Canada, New Zealand, and the United States are all built on
migrants of this type and there were periods in each case when
the governments offered incentives for people to *immigrate*. After
World War II, Britain too lodged advertisements in a number of
former colonies for people with specific skills, such as nursing
and engineering, to come and help to rebuild the country when
such skills were in short supply. It was from this time, then, that
immigrant communities from the West Indies, Africa, and the
Indian sub-continent began to establish themselves in Britain.

There have been many useful anthropological studies of the
experience of such immigrants. Oxford anthropologist Alison
Shaw's excellent in-depth focus on three generations of Pakistani
settlers in Oxford, England, raises many of the issues that perme-
ate the literature. The community is still quite contained, for
example, and retains ties with the specific part of Pakistan from
which many members of the Oxford community hail. Thus, new
arrivals can draw on a web of support from those with a longer
experience in the UK, and the Pakistani community can offer
links with their heritage for those born in Oxford, even to the
extent of providing spouses for them. The immigrant community
in Oxford has built a series of shops to serve their needs, as well
as gradually improving their facilities for worship, a beautiful new
mosque now adding a distinctive architectural feature to the area
where they predominate. At the same time, two generations of
children have grown up in Oxford and have established ties with

other members of the community, so the settlement patterns have diversified, as have relations with neighbouring families.

A second reason why people leave their own countries is because they find themselves on the wrong side of a political divide, perhaps during or following a civil war, or because they oppose the ideals of a regime in power. Perhaps facing arrest, persecution, discrimination, or violence, they seek to escape and build new lives elsewhere. There is another huge anthropological literature on the plight of such *refugees*, who may also be described as *asylum seekers*, this time examining the way that people rebuild an identity for themselves, but nevertheless seek to retain important elements of their cultural foundations. A classic work in this field is Renée Hirschon's study *Heirs of the Greek Catastrophe*, which follows a community of refugees who were relocated after the war between Greece and Turkey in 1921–22 to the city of Piraeus, Greece. The members of the community share a language, culture, and religion with their fellow residents of Greece, but through the generations they have retained a distinctive Asia Minor identity based on family, neighbourhood, and deep religious convictions.

A third important aspect of the movement of people is the phenomenon of travelling on a short-term basis to work or study in another country. Economic factors often play a part here too, so one member of a family may travel abroad to work, but send his or her spare earnings home, perhaps to save for a specific purpose such as buying a house, or starting a business. People at the other end of the economic ladder, who are already earning well, may choose to send their children abroad to study, perhaps to broaden their experience, or to give them an edge over others when they enter the job market. The travellers in either case may choose to settle in the new location, and anthropological work also addresses these situations, including reactions from the host community. Women from the Philippines are a good example of people who travel abroad to work, at first temporarily, and the Japanese anthropologist Nobue Suzuki has spent several years examining various possible outcomes in the case of those who chose Tokyo as a destination.

Travel and tourism

Travelling as a form of education or recreation is another explanation for the movement of people, but the widespread version of this practice that has become known as *tourism* is a relatively new response to technological change. As rapid forms of transport have developed and opened up much of the world for prices many people can afford, at least occasionally, there has been a profound impact on those who inhabit popular destinations. The anthropology of tourism has focused on the effects of this enormous international industry at very local levels, seeking to measure the economic benefits, but also calculating the price of social and cultural change. It has examined the extent to which cultural difference has become part of the tourist attraction of a location, the degree of playful interaction that is possible between 'hosts' and 'guests' as a kind of rite of passage, especially for young people, and the impact of experiencing cultural variety in the places which source the visitors. A valuable early collection entitled *Hosts and Guests*, edited by Valene Smith, has been reprinted and revisited several times since it was first published in 1977.

Like the colonization and international trade we have just discussed, there is often an economic disparity between hosts and tourists, and this can have a serious effect on relations between the different peoples involved. Typically, tourists from a rich nation travel to a place where it is relatively cheap to buy goods and services, and while some of the local people may benefit from the influx of wealth the tourists bring, it is usually governments and the multinational hotel chains that gain the most. These economic benefits often override other claims to locations that tourists find attractive, and an informative book entitled

Figure 9.1 The famous Inca site at Machu Picchu is popular with tourists and brings in a substantial income to the Peruvian government, but it is reported that the local indigenous people have lost control of its protection and are often treated badly by the visitors.
© Jim Nicholson / Alamy

Is the Sacred for Sale, by Alison Johnston, offers many examples of the detrimental effect on places considered sacred by local people. Two well-known cases involve the extraordinary feature in Australia known by visitors as Ayers Rock, but *Uluru* to the Anangu Aboriginal people, who find the popular activity of climbing on the rock distressing. The other is Machu Picchu in Peru, where the local Quechua-speaking people would like to visit the site in the silence they feel is appropriate to this sacred place, but during the week it is too expensive and on Sunday, when access is free, it is too noisy.

A more recent anthropological approach to tourism has set out to examine the extent to which people *act out* or *perform* cultural differences for the purpose of attracting visitors, and whether these performances can then be considered to be an *authentic* experience for the tourist. The presence of foreign guests is anywhere a kind of trigger to consider how much our lives represent local cultural features, and we may also exaggerate what we think is the appropriate way to behave in our own society simply to make a good impression. This kind of intercultural encounter is also a time for examining one's own identity, and if residents of a place that has become a tourist resort choose to enact their cultural heritage, even if only for visitors, this would seem to be yet another example of cultural revival; in fact, it might even be considered a kind of *cultural capital,* since they are taking advantage of others' interest in their heritage. University of Sheffield anthropologist Simone Abram has written about the subtle differences chosen by people in the Auvergne, in France, when acting out their history, first for tourists, then for more local visitors. A study of Bali by the Japanese anthropologist Shinji Yamashita looks at the way Balinese both act out their own identity for visitors to their islands, and at the same time express their differences from the wider Indonesian nation of which they also form a part.

The spread of technological change

A characteristic feature of the anthropological studies of the last few decades is their need to take account of the access to the internet that even some of the most geographically isolated people now enjoy. This technological advance has opened up the world to information that was previously only available to those with comparatively high levels of education or economic power. No longer is the anthropologist the only person who knows about people living in formerly inaccessible areas. Together with the wider distribution of goods and of the people who market them, these technological changes have transformed the lives of a vast range of peoples around the world. It would be a grave mistake, however, to imagine that all who access such information understand it in the same way. An important element of these anthropological studies, therefore, remains the way in which the world differs depending on the local situation from which it is viewed.

One of the consequences of satellite and internet communications is the ability to express identity to others virtually, not just in person. This has transformed groups known as *diaspora* – geographically scattered peoples who share a common cultural identity. They previously maintained this identity through memory and ritual practice, but now they can gather online and do this in more direct ways. One anthropological study of this kind of community was that conducted by London anthropologists Daniel Miller and Don Slater, focusing on the communication of 'Trinis', all people who hail at some point from Trinidad. In their book *The Internet: An Ethnographic Approach* they discuss characteristics of this online community such as the use of quite esoteric language and the replication virtually of some of the practices of actually meeting in Trinidad known as *liming*, involving banter about music, food, and sex. An early virtual bookshop was another feature, as well as chat rooms, pen pal services, and a magazine called Kalypso.

This kind of virtual community is rather common nowadays for people all over the world who don't necessarily share an identity, but who communicate through a common interest in various forms of activity. Facebook is one highly successful example, first taken up especially by young people, and there is also an academic equivalent called Academia.edu which allows people with similar research interests instantly to follow each other's plans and publications as they enter them into the system.

Studies of these types of community have revealed a negative aspect of making one's life so public and accessible, however. For example, activities which it seemed amusing to share as a school pupil, or student, may not look impressive to a prospective employer searching the internet for background information about an applicant, or when a potential politician seeks to impress his or her constituents. Academics also change their minds and they can find it limiting, or even embarrassing, to have an old out-of-date article coming up first every time someone 'Googles' their name.

A popular approach to the new worlds of people connected by virtual means, and moving rather freely across national borders, is that of the Swedish anthropologist Ulf Hannerz who has written extensively about what he calls *transnational connections*. As well as people linked through ethnicity, or perhaps former residence or religion, transnational connections are again often made through a shared occupation or interest. One of Hannerz's own research projects was with foreign correspondents, communicating news to readers in many different nations but all based in the same city in which he got to know them. Another Swedish study, by Helena Wulff, looks at dance in the same transnational context, in this case focusing on ballet. She uses an ethnographic perspective to bring the reader right into the heart of the world of ballet dancers, wherever they are, while at the same time demonstrating ways in which a formerly local or 'national' approach has gradually been replaced by a need to be flexible enough to work in a global or transnational context.

Local impact

In the previous chapter, we noted that some projects instituted by rich nations and colonial powers may not have beneficial effects for everyone concerned. When governments introduce big projects to achieve economic goals on a national level, they may even have *detrimental* effects at the local level. One of the roles anthropologists can play is to help local people make their voices heard in a world that has − until recently − been beyond their ability to challenge. Because anthropologists who work in the area gain a deep knowledge of local peoples, and possibly have a better knowledge of the outside world, they can act as advocates, or at least advisers. Former colonial powers have for decades been sending aid to the countries they once occupied, with a variety of reactions and results at the local level, and anthropologists have been involved both as facilitators of the aid programmes, and again as advocates for the supposed recipients of the aid. In between the donors and the receivers stand government officials who may have their own ideas about the aid required in their nations, and who are sometimes accused of siphoning off the income in directions that conflict with the original intentions.

An example of the first case, which is well known in the anthropological literature and beyond, has been the collective reaction of the Kayapo people of the Amazonian rain forest to various projects of the Brazilian government, as reported and encouraged by the Cornell University anthropologist Terence Turner. The citing of a proposed dam was an initial shock for them as it would inundate and make useless a great swathe of their traditional lands, and negotiations followed about how its location could be better worked out. A great contribution of the anthropologist in this case was to bring in a film crew to record the agreements as there had been other cases in which compensation promised to local people for such ventures had never materialized. The Kayapo soon learned to use the video cameras themselves and they could make sure that all discussions were recorded in a way that they could understand. There are some interesting films about this situation, but it is, of course, only one of many examples of exploitation of the lands of the Indigenous peoples of the South American rain forests.

The building of dams and the associated displacement of peoples has been a common phenomenon around the world as nations work out ways to provide facilities for their growing urban conurbations and big industrial ventures. Clearly, everyone needs water, and it is sometimes possible to persuade those affected adversely to co-operate by offering other benefits. One example was a dam on the Saru River, in Hokkaido in the north of Japan, which would divert the traditional salmon breeding grounds of the Ainu people who had lived there long before the majority Japanese population were sent to settle in cities like Sapporo. Salmon used to form their staple diet, and so there was opposition to the idea, even though the Ainu now have access to other food. The community of Nibutani, which would be most affected by the project, was split over the decision, and although the dam construction went ahead, it is possible to this day to see the result of that division in the two separate museums that represent Ainu culture there. One is a spacious modern building with all sorts of up-to-date facilities, financed by the dam construction project; the other an old-fashioned but rather more scholarly museum set up by a local Ainu activist who dedicated his life to collecting Ainu materials.

The technological advances that have made such enormous ventures possible are applied to any number of other projects that will apparently be beneficial to the wider population of a nation, but there has been a global backlash which may also be having a detrimental effect on local people. This is somewhat ironically concerned with *conservation* – of lands, trees, and all kinds of other living beings, in a nutshell of *biodiversity* – but which sometimes neglects the human beings who inhabit an area under consideration. The wider project is often couched in terms of *sustainable development* which, like *ecological tourism*, sounds rather positive, but the effects at a local level are often much more complicated. The book *Conservation and Mobile Indigenous Peoples: Displacement, Forced Settlement and Sustainable Development* examines no fewer than twenty-one cases across many countries of peoples being forced to relocate in the interest of sustainable development. One of the editors, Marcus Colchester, is an anthropologist who works full-time with Indigenous peoples who find themselves in situations of environmental conflict.

There are also many examples of difficulties with projects installed with the ostensible aim of offering aid directly to people who are perceived to need it. The perception is sometimes ill-judged from the level of the government or NGO offering the aid; it is also sometimes linked to political directives – an example that reached the international press being the aid offered by the Japanese government to countries that supported whaling – but there are also a number of difficulties on the ground with misunderstandings at a very local level. For example, recall the clinic that was trying to prevent HIV/AIDS in India but failed to find appropriate language to discuss the issues, and so had trouble getting their messages across at all. Similarly, agricultural developments are often introduced that conflict with local indigenous knowledge and so are spurned. It is only recently that anyone but anthropologists has taken seriously the value of indigenous knowledge, and this has at last begun to transform the whole endeavour of so-called development.

Resistance among indigenous peoples

Another powerful example of a global process that has arisen alongside the revitalization of cultural difference is the co-operation of Indigenous peoples around the world to support each other in their efforts to reclaim the cultural heritage they lost during the colonization of their lands. Several standing committees have been set up at the United Nations to deal with aspects of this venture, but there has also been a great deal of informal support through exchanges of cultural activities such as theatre and dance. The internet has facilitated much communication and publicity and *Natives on the Net,* edited by Kyra Landzelius, offers cases from as far apart as Greenland and Aboriginal Australia, on topics as diverse as e-health and language revival.

The loss of indigenous language has been one of the issues that most concerns people, largely for the way that it embodies and explains a lot of the culture that they share. It also is a powerful identity marker, and strong efforts are being made in many parts of the world to revitalize languages and pass them on to younger generations before they disappear. A particular bone of contention has been the assimilation policies that were administered by many colonial powers, which set up residential schools to train Native children to shake off their heritage and learn to be citizens of the new colony. These children were often punished for using their Native languages.

The plan backfired, especially in North America, because children from formerly warring tribes realized that they were all being subjected to the same oppressive system, and in the 1960s the Red Power movement grew precisely among the graduates of such schools. The film *Rabbit Proof Fence,* about three small girls who escaped from a residential school in Australia, became internationally acclaimed, and in 2008, the Australian prime minister apologized to the 'stolen generations' whose heritage had been removed in this way.

In some areas, land claims form part of this movement, as mentioned earlier. Some of the First Nations have never signed a treaty with the Canadian government and still claim their own territory. The Haida people who live in islands that were named after Queen Charlotte offer one example, and these lands have now been renamed Haida Gwaii. This concession only happened after long periods of suffering, however, and decimation of the original population through diseases such as smallpox inflicted on them by the colonizing visitors. Other First Nations must prove that the land was once theirs, and to do this they sometimes enlist the help of archaeologists to unearth artefacts to provide material proof. First Nations whose land has been completely urbanized can in some cases claim a percentage of the profits when land changes hands, and the Squamish people who live in Vancouver have achieved such an arrangement.

Another aspect of the revitalization of these ancient cultures is the increasing recognition of the value of the tried and tested indigenous knowledge to scientists who previously dismissed the ideas they heard as old wives' tales and superstition. Pharmaceutical companies have for many years been trawling the rain forests and other indigenous lands for drugs they can develop and market, and founder of the Body Shop, Anita Roddick, used many native

Figure 9.2 Peasants and coca producers take part in the national day of mass chewing of coca leaves in La Paz, Bolivia, 12 March 2012. The rally seeks to support Bolivian President Evo Morales in his intention of de-criminalization and de-penalization of the coca leaf.
© epa European pressphoto agency b.v. / Alamy

ideas in the development of her beauty products. Medical practitioners have taken longer to be convinced, but some of the so-called alter (native) therapies can be traced to indigenous sources. The election of the former coca-growers' union leader Evo Morales as president of Bolivia has opened up a whole series of plans to 'indigenize' national ventures.

The human biology of the future

Biological anthropology is a subject that might at first appear to be primarily concerned with the past and perhaps lacking in modern applications. In fact, nothing could be further from the truth. The continuing study of our evolutionary past reveals not just more about how we differ from our primate cousins, but also the significant amount we share. The old ideas about humans being somehow separate or superior to other animals have been swept away and we now understand that we form an integral part of a much wider ecosystem that extends across the whole planet. Biological anthropology also includes a wide range of different fields such as human palaeontology, evolutionary biology, human genetics, comparative anatomy and physiology, primate behaviour, human behavioural ecology, and human biology (modern human biological variation, human ecology, nutrition, and demography). In exploring the human species biological anthropology helps us to understand the causes of current human diversity.

The twenty-first century promises to be an exciting time for the discipline. Our understanding of the genetics of extinct human species such as the Neanderthals is gathering pace and the 2011 discovery of 'Species X' or the Denisova hominin in the Altai Mountains of Siberia is surely the first of many new species to be identified through genetics rather than anatomical description – a situation unthinkable even twenty years ago.

Similarly, our picture of early hominin evolution continues to become more advanced with every new fossil discovery, while advances in dating techniques allow us to attach ever firmer dates to our distant ancestors and the material remains they left behind. The search for *Homo sapiens* dispersal route out of Africa should also yield new data as different strands of information, from archaeology, genetics, and climate records from the past, are more effectively combined to present a detailed picture of our journey.

Our relationship to the other primates and the wider environment is another area that continues to develop in importance. Human population growth is increasingly bringing people into contact and conflict with non-human primates and other animal species. How best to manage this problem, delicately balancing the importance of conservation with the need to grow crops or develop infrastructures, engages many biological anthropologists. There is no simple answer but much practical work is being undertaken to ease the problem through better management, education, and tourism programmes. Work in this area has also shown that human behaviours such as the trade in bush meat (eating forest dwelling animals such as primates) have brought people into contact with diseases that crossed over from non-human primates. For instance, it is now generally accepted that HIV/AIDS jumped to humans from gorillas when their carcases were butchered for meat. The increase in the trade in bush meat has gone hand in hand with the movement of human populations from rural to urban areas. As the urban population increases so too does the need for food, which in turn places greater pressure on undeveloped land. This process has received much attention in South America through the destruction of the Amazon rainforest, but the problem is equally acute in Africa and Asia.

Biological anthropologists are also actively working at combating problems facing the developing world such as poor nutrition and disease. For example, education programmes aimed at malarial regions emphasize the importance of keeping mosquito nets repaired, while studies of nutrition in countries such as Bangladesh are combating the impact of parasitic diseases on children's development by seeking a better understanding of how specific parasites block the body's uptake of nutrients. The combined approach of the scientific study of people and practical action allows biological anthropologists to make a very real improvement in people's lives.

The second half of the last century also saw a much better understanding of the transmission of diseases between populations. Today, we are all familiar with the dangers posed by the possible mutations of the H1N1 flu virus (especially the avian and swine forms). However, in the past anthropologists keen to make contact with 'undiscovered' peoples often brought with them lethal diseases such as smallpox and measles, against which these groups had no natural immunity. Sadly, in the past, human lives and much human diversity were deliberately eradicated through evil and immoral business practices that included the intentional infection of indigenous groups through the 'gift' of blankets contaminated with disease. Tragically, Indigenous peoples were often seen as standing in the way of profit – a terrible example was the case of Brazil's *Serviço de Proteção aos Índios* (Indian Protection Service). Although initially it did much for indigenous rights, its mission was subverted and it came actively to encourage the extermination of the people it was charged with protecting. It was disbanded in 1967 and a wave of prosecutions followed but it was estimated that between 1900 and 1967 at least ninety-eight separate tribes were wiped out in Brazil alone. Today, strict rules are in place to prevent contact with the last few remaining tribes that shun links with the outside world and tight controls prevent the transmission of diseases common in the general human population but deadly to those who have no natural immunity – a slight positive legacy for an horrific chapter in the story of human contact.

As noted above, travel and the immediacy of global communication have made our world seem a smaller place. Certainly we are now able to travel distances in a few hours that the first humans to leave Africa would not have been able to conceptualize while modern telecommunications now mean that it is possible to get an internet connection at the summit of Mount Everest. However, biological anthropology retains a crucial role in allowing us increasingly to understand what it is to be human. It gives us a sense of how we have become human from studying our evolution, how we vary by studying our differences, and what we share in common with other organisms on our planet. But perhaps the greatest thing that biological anthropology makes us confront is what we share with each other.

10
Practising anthropology

Finally, we will turn to the initial subject of this book: how anthropology is practised. We will consider the methods used by anthropologists to gain an understanding of the unity and diversity of peoples that inhabit our shared world and examine how these have been modified to accommodate the technological change we discussed in the last two chapters. We will also suggest ways that students of the subject may put into practice some of the methods we have described, particularly in light of the relationship between anthropologists and the people with whom they work, in other words, the *ethics* of doing anthropological research. Methods such as *participant observation* and *interviews* will be considered, with close attention being paid to the importance of involving those who are being researched in the whole endeavour. Mention will be made of the variety of anthropologies that now exist in different parts of the world, and attempts that are being made to bring them together. Finally, we will evaluate the importance of anthropology in the modern world and look to the role it may play in the future.

Going into the field

The characteristic feature of anthropological research, especially that of social and cultural anthropologists, is the *time* spent *in the field* and the degree of involvement with those who form the focus of our interest. This method is known as *participant observation*, sometimes referred to in other disciplines as *ethnographic* research, but most professional anthropologists spend at least a year, sometimes a lifetime, albeit interrupted from time to time, living and working with the people they choose as their focus. This enables an incredibly high degree of understanding, especially when the research takes place over the long term, and the value of the method should never be underestimated. The research will be peppered with *interviews*, especially *unstructured* ones that allow new ideas to emerge, and many anthropologists make or use *questionnaires* and numerical *surveys* to add a broader context to their findings. However, while all of these tools are useful, intensive *participation* in a society's workings – from the daily serving of food to special rites of passage – is the real heart (or salt) of the anthropological encounter.

There are several aspects to this kind of work. Let us start with the *researcher*, in practice the chief *tool* of the investigation. Social anthropological research is a case of human beings working with other human beings to gain an understanding of their ways of thinking, so the whole business is built on the *relationships* that comprise the learning process. There is no way that this research can be carried out in a completely *objective* manner; indeed, it is through getting to know people *subjectively*, in a personal way, that one best learns what one needs to know. It is necessary, therefore, to adopt a *reflexive* attitude to one's experience, to examine exactly how one is absorbing the local behaviour, and how one's prior experience might influence the findings. *Anthropology and Autobiography,* a collection of essays edited by Judith Okely and Helen Callaway, offers many useful examples of this experience – including one from this book's co-author Joy Hendry – about the difficulties of combining friendship with research in the field. These issues are analysed more theoretically by the British anthropologist Charlotte Aull Davies in her book *Reflexive Ethnography*.

A person who decides to take up anthropology as a lifetime career often gets involved in a deep and long-term way with the people we used to call our *informants*, and at the same time, they may become some of those we know best in the world. We thus become acutely aware of their humanity, just as we need to notice our own human qualities and limitations in the way we do the research. A more recent term that has been used to describe those who help us in our work is *collaborator*. It takes more account of the degree of involvement of such people, and the extent to which we become indebted to them. The more we build up *mutual respect* at a local level, however, the more we may be open to criticisms from other disciplines of *going native* and failing to adopt what they regard as a suitable degree of analytical rigour – factors that definitely need to be addressed.

Figure 10.1 Joy Hendry (and son and baby sitter) attending a sea festival in Japan. The Shinto priest behind her is preparing the float to be carried out to sea.

One of the advantages of studying anthropology at school, in university, or with friends and colleagues of different backgrounds, is that you can work through some of these issues together. You may already have good relationships that are not built on the *researcher/ researched* division that tends to put the one being researched in an inferior position, due to a lack of the knowledge and training that the researcher brings to the encounter. Working together you can both bring your learning to the meeting and proceed on a basis of prior shared understanding that takes a huge amount of time for an outside anthropologist to build up in a new location. Learning anthropology within a multicultural community is a great way to overcome the historical legacy of inequality that we discussed in the introduction to this book, and to enable the formation of a new discipline that is much more fairly shared than in the past. At the same time, the fairer approach may help to rebuild relations with displaced Indigenous peoples, as discussed in chapters 8 and 9.

Ultimately, we are talking about the *ethics* of doing research with other human beings, and although much has been written about this subject too, it is a good principle to bear in mind that if you treat the people with whom you work in a way that would be acceptable to you, were you in their situation, you will have made a good start. Here we see again that old rule of reciprocity, and a second issue to consider is what you are giving back to the community that is helping you with your research. Among scholars of Indigenous studies it is a *sine qua non* that research should bring benefit to the community where it is carried out. This idea is explained in the influential book *Decolonizing Methodologies* by the Māori scholar Linda Tuhiwai Smith, who also makes clear how demeaning it may feel to be the 'object' of research. Of course, the wider aim of enabling international understanding may not seem as valuable to those deeply entrenched in a local environment as it does to an anthropologist operating in a global arena. The websites set up by several professional bodies, including the American Anthropological Association and the Association of Social Anthropologists of Great Britain and the Commonwealth, run through these issues in detail.

Considering 'the other'

All the time spent gathering information would certainly be of little use if anthropologists didn't share it, and after completing fieldwork the next task is to work out how to transmit and explain what we have learned to our colleagues and, preferably, the wider public. Very often anthropologists do their research in a different language to their own, which is quite helpful when it comes to explanation because the task becomes one of *translation*. Thought must be given to systems of *classification* and the other issues discussed earlier in this book. Even if an anthropologist chooses to work in his or her own language, members of different groups may use it differently. Consider the variations in the use of English found in America and Australia, for example, or simply in different dialects within the same country. Consider also the ways in which language varies from one generation to another, or between groups with different levels of formal education. Translating these differences is another task of an anthropologist.

These issues apply to the way anthropologists speak about, or write up their findings, and what we produce is called *ethnography*, literally the writings about a particular *ethnos* or group of people. Other ways of representing the findings might be through images such as photographs and sketches, in sound recordings, perhaps of music or song, and in video clips and various kinds of film. In all cases, the author needs to consider what to include in the account and in what order, how to select and arrange the images, and what shots to pick to make a good film. In short, we need to consider *how* to *represent* the people concerned, and the message we want to portray. Again, this is hardly an *objective* matter, and collaboration can help: for writing, to check that we have properly understood what we are recounting, and that we are quoting people accurately; in photographs, to ensure that our subjects are happy with their images; and for film ... one recently popular method is to hand a camera to people with whom we work in the field and allow them to select the images to shoot.

We also need to consider the audience at whom our representations are directed. If it is purely academic, we can assume a certain level of comparative knowledge, for example, and we can place our findings in an existing theoretical context. If it includes members of the group of people we studied, they will have an inside understanding of what we are representing, indeed they might disagree with our interpretation. If we are addressing complete strangers, we might find it hard to predict what kind of approach to take. One teacher of anthropology in Hong Kong, Grant Evans, complained that many writers assume they are addressing an American or European readership, even if they are writing about Asia, and forget that the subject is taught worldwide. He produced a collected volume, *Asia's Cultural Mosaic*, for which each contributor was asked to think about Evans's Chinese students as they wrote. Since that time, anthropologists have been debating the variations in the way their subject is studied, as well as taught and represented, according to where they are in the world.

Here lies another important ethical issue then. In the early days of anthropology, the communities would be rather separate, and a field site for Europeans would typically be in a distant land, requiring long and sometimes quite arduous travel to reach it. Once they returned, follow-up communication was slow and difficult, if not impossible, and anthropologists were only required to explain their findings to colleagues who shared their training and publication language. Even in North American and colonial universities, an educational barrier tended to maintain this distinction between the community of research and that of representation. Nowadays, technology of communication is not the only dramatic change; the broad spread of educational opportunities has opened up the former ivory towers of learning to people in many walks of life, and scholars need to consider that their representations are rather likely to reach their field collaborators.

For the biological anthropologist there are a number of ethical issues that must be considered when undertaking research. A prime example is the use of human remains. Many of the large skeletal collections held by European and American museums were assembled during the nineteenth and early twentieth centuries in ways that would now be considered totally unacceptable. However, study of these same skeletons has allowed many old-fashioned ideas about race and the perceived superiority of one population over another to be shown to be utter nonsense. The tragic irony is that the skeletons were often collected to prop up Victorian and Edwardian ideas about European superiority but modern study shows the reverse. Some indigenous groups have taken legal action to have the bones of their ancestors returned to them for reburial. However, other groups are happy for the material to be studied so long as the bones are treated with respect. It is a delicate ethical issue for the biological anthropologist and one that continues to inflame strong opinions if not handled with care and respect. Similarly, care must be taken during fieldwork that Western researchers do not parachute in to fieldwork sites and undermine the work of local scientists. Thankfully, within the field of human evolution there is an internationally agreed protocol that prevents fossils being removed from the country within which they were discovered. This has led to large amounts of, often Western, money being used to develop and sustain the scientific infrastructure of countries that would otherwise not benefit if the fossils were whisked away to America or Paris.

Figure 10.2 Tracing early human movements across the Arabian Peninsula, Simon Underdown (right) and colleagues take a break from the 40°C heat in Dhofar desert, Oman.

Evidence versus interpretation

In both biological and social anthropology, the role of the scholar is to use the evidence collected not only to explain, but also to *interpret* the materials in the broader context of training in the various theoretical approaches of the subject – even perhaps to move theory forward, or to propose new ideas. This is the level at which social or cultural anthropologists may need to move beyond what collaborators can assist with – unless of course both have been trained together, as proposed above. By now, we have examined various theories about the biological development of human behaviour, and the tendency of social and cultural life to conform to general principles that have been identified over years of study. Thus, the materials gathered – artefacts, language,

symbolism, daily activities, ritual behaviour – all need to be analysed in this broader context.

For biological anthropology, evidence can come from an
often bewildering number of distinct sources. To interpret
properly the site of a fossil requires the use of anatomy, geology,
physics, and biology to name but a few disciplines. Once we have
begun to piece together the data the next stage is interpretation.
Within biological anthropology and especially human evolution
we interpret material within the context of evolutionary process.
This means that when looking at a fossil we try to understand the
process that led to a particular adaptation evolving. For instance,
we can see very clearly the way in which bipedalism (walking on
two legs) evolved in hominins. But in order to interpret this
properly we need to try to explain why evolution was favouring
or selecting for this ability and within biological anthropology
this is frankly where the fun begins. There are many theories as
to *why* bipedalism evolved, some are more likely than others but
we face the problem of sorting the good ideas from the bad to
create a working model of interpretation. As new pieces of data
are added, the model is revised or sometimes completely aban-
doned in favour of a better model. In this way, we develop our
understanding of the processes that shaped our evolution and
created the diversity that we see in ourselves today.

For a social or cultural anthropologist, evidence may also lie
in artefacts. The advantage to engaging in *participant observation* is
that we can see how objects are made, ask about their meanings,
and observe them being used in ritual, or in daily life. We can
discuss their value with people, we can see how they fit into a
broader context of activity, and we can listen to how they are
referenced in speech, or in other forms of communication, such
as gift exchange and aesthetic, religious, or artistic frames. Ritual
is a rich source of evidence for theories we might make about
social and cultural life, and the symbolism of each element of a
ritual will help us to make interpretations of the whole event

within the wider social context. For all these reasons, anthropologists need to keep very careful and detailed notes so that they can work through them together, after an event is over, and see how they fit into the broader, *holistic* picture of life in a particular society.

In Hendry's own research in Japan, initially about polite language, she found that there were parallels to the various linguistic expressions she observed in the *wrapping* of gifts, in the way that people dress for particular occasions, in the style of arranging space – from offices to tea rooms – and in the organization of people, for example in a ritual, a parade, or a military retinue. The term for wrapping – wrapping of space, wrapping of objects, wrapping of the body, and the wrapping of words, can be translated directly into English, but the overall meaning is different. In the English usage, we associate wrapping with the covering, or concealing of something inside the wrapping and our chief aim is usually to remove it and reveal the contents. In the Japanese situation, much of the communication is to be found in the wrapping itself, and to remove it without understanding this, would be to miss the whole point. Hendry's book on this subject gives examples of other cultures in which this form is used in further ways, but this is just one example of how an anthropologist can make the familiar strange, and therefore help to make the strange familiar.

The value of anthropology

The findings of anthropologists are not only valuable in the academic world, but potentially could provide a tremendous resource for policy makers, businesspeople, politicians, and those engaged in international affairs. At present, different nations use anthropologists to different degrees. In Norway, they are rather well regarded, they are consulted quite regularly, and they are asked to make comments on various issues in public arenas such as television. Similarly in Japan, anthropologists contribute to the understanding of business and leisure in a variety of sometimes quite amusing outlets. The Norwegian anthropologist Thomas Hylland Eriksen has written an excellent book challenging anthropologists in other nations to work harder to make a contribution to all these fields. 'Anthropologists should have changed the world', he writes ... 'should have been at the forefront of public debate about multiculturalism and nationalism, the human aspects of information technology, poverty and economic globalization, human rights issues ... just to mention a few topical areas.'

The operative word here is 'should', for there is still a lot of work to do, and the major contribution that anthropology can make still lies ahead. The official introduction of anthropology in English schools in 2010 could be an important step in the right direction, for the younger people are when they learn about the subject, the more likely they are to use it in practical ways. At present there are many good anthropologists, but too many of them talk to each other, and fail to get the message out to the wider world. One of the chief aims of this guide is to respond to Eriksen's challenge and open the field of anthropology to a wider readership.

Further reading

1 The human body

Blacking, John (1977). *The Anthropology of the Body* (ASA Monograph no. 15). London, New York, and San Francisco: Academic Press.

Diamond, Jared (2006). *The Third Chimpanzee: The Evolution and Future of the Human Animal*. London: Harper Perennial.

Gould, Stephen Jay (1981). *The Mismeasure of Man*. London: Penguin Books. (A lively account of the uses and abuses of intelligence quotient (IQ) testing.)

Hertz, Robert (1973). 'The Pre-eminence of the Right Hand: A Study in Religious Polarity', in Rodney Needham (ed.), *Left and Right*. Chicago: University of Chicago Press.

Leach, Edmund (1966). 'Animal Categories and Verbal Abuse' in Eric H. Lenneberg (ed.), *New Directions for the Study of Language*. Cambridge, Mass.: MIT Press.

Leroi, Armand Marie (2005). *Mutants: On the Form, Varieties and Errors of the Human Body*. London: Harper Perennial.

Mauss, Marcel (1973). 'Techniques of the Body.' *Economy and Society* 2 (1): 70–88.

Ucko, Peter J. (1969). *Penis Sheaths: A Comparative Study* (The Curl Lecture). London: Royal Anthropological Institute of Great Britain and Ireland.

2 Ways of thinking and communicating

Burling, Robbins (2005). *The Talking Ape: How Language Evolved*. Oxford: Oxford University Press.

Carroll, John B. (ed.) (1997). *Language, Thought, and Reality: Selected Writings of Benjamin Lee Whorf.* Cambridge, Mass.: MIT Press.

Christensen, Pia, Jenny Hockey, and Allison James (2001). 'Talk, Silence and the Material World: Patterns of Indirect Communication among Agricultural Families in Northern England' in Joy Hendry and C. W. Watson (eds.). *An Anthropology of Indirect Communication.* London and New York: Routledge.

Deacon, Terrence (1998). *The Symbolic Species: The Co-Evolution of Language and the Human Brain.* London: Penguin Books.

Dunbar, Robin (1997). *Grooming, Gossip, and the Evolution of Language.* Cambridge, Mass.: Harvard University Press.

Durkheim, Emile, and Marcel Mauss (1963). *Primitive Classification,* transl. with introduction by Rodney Needham. London: Cohen & West.

Evans-Pritchard, E. E. (1976). *Witchcraft, Oracles and Magic among the Azande.* Oxford: Clarendon Press.

Howe, James, and Joel Sherzer (1986). 'Friend Hairyfish and Friend Rattlesnake: Or Keeping Anthropologists in their Place.' *Man* 21: 680–96.

Lambert, Helen (2001). 'Not Talking about Sex in India: Indirection and the Communication of Bodily Intention' in Joy Hendry and C. W. Watson (eds). *An Anthropology of Indirect Communication.* London and New York: Routledge.

Needham, Rodney (1979). *Symbolic Classification,* Santa Monica, Calif.: Goodyear Publishing Company.

3 Organizing social relations

Baumann, Gerd (1996). *Contesting Culture: Discourses of Identity in Multiethnic London.* Cambridge: Cambridge University Press.

Dumont, Louis (1980). *Homo Hierarchicus: The Caste System and Its Implications.* Chicago: University of Chicago Press.

Freeman, Luke (2007). 'Why Are Some People Powerful?' in Rita Astuti, Jonathan P. Parry, and Charles Stafford (eds). *Questions of Anthropology.* Oxford: Berg Publishers.

Gellner, David N., and Declan Quigley (eds) (1995). *Contested Hierarchies: A Collaborative Ethnography of Caste among the Newars of the Kathmandu Valley, Nepal*. Oxford: Clarendon Press.

Hamabata, Matthews Masayuki (1990). *Crested Kimono: Power and Love in the Japanese Business Family*. Cornell, N.Y.: Cornell University Press.

Malinowski, Bronisław (1922). *Argonauts of the Western Pacific*. London: Routledge & Kegan Paul.

Mauss, Marcel (1970). *The Gift,* transl. by I. Cunnison. London: Cohen & West.

Quigley, Declan (1993). *The Interpretation of Caste*. Oxford: Oxford University Press.

Walker, Alan, and Shipman, Pat (1996). *The Wisdom of the Bones: In Search of Human Origins*. London: Weidenfeld & Nicolson.

Weiner, Annette B. (1992). *Inalienable Possessions: The Paradox of Keeping-While-Giving*. Berkeley: University of California Press.

Wilson, Monica (1983, originally published 1951). *Good Company: A Study of Nyakyusa Age-villages*. Westport, Conn.: Greenwood Press.

4 Engaging with nature

Asquith, Pamela J., and Arne Kalland (eds) (1997). *Japanese Images of Nature*. Richmond, UK: Curzon Press.

Barnard, Alan (2007). *Anthropology and the Bushman*. Oxford and New York: Berg.

Cajete, Gregory (2000). *Native Science: Natural Laws of Interdependence*. Santa Fe, New Mexico: Clear Light Publishers.

Dawkins, Richard (2005). *The Ancestor's Tale: A Pilgrimage to the Dawn of Life*. London: Phoenix.

Gamble, Clive (2003). *Timewalkers: The Prehistory of Global Colonisation*. London: History Press.

Ingold, Tim (2000). *The Perception of the Environment*. Abingdon: Routledge.

O'Biso, Carol. (1987). *First Light: A Magical Journey*. Auckland, New Zealand: Reed. (A moving personal account by an American curator of her experience working with Māori wooden sculptures.)

Ortner, Sherry B. (1974). 'Is Female to Male as Nature Is to Culture?' in M. Z. Rosaldo and L. Lamphere (eds). *Woman, Culture and Society*. Stanford, Calif.: Stanford University Press.

Lewin, Roger, and Robert Foley (2004). *Principles of Human Evolution*. Oxford: Blackwell.

Moran, Emilio (2008). *Human Adaptability, An Introduction to Ecological Anthropology*. Philadelphia, Penn.: Westview Press.

Morphy, Howard (1991). *Ancestral Connections: Art and an Aboriginal System of Knowledge*. Chicago: University of Chicago Press.

Ridley, Matt (1994). *The Red Queen: Sex and Evolution of Human Nature*. London: Penguin.

Strathern Marilyn (1992). *After Nature: English Kinship in the Late Twentieth Century*. Cambridge: Cambridge University Press.

—— (1980). 'No Nature, No Culture: The Hagen Case' in Carol MacCormack and Marilyn Strathern (eds). *Nature, Culture and Gender*. Cambridge: Cambridge University Press.

5 Personhood

Barth, Fredrik (1966). *Models of Social Organisation* (Occasional Paper no. 23). London: Royal Anthropological Institute.

Berreman, Gerald (1962). *Behind Many Masks: Ethnography and Impression Management in a Himalayan Village* (Monograph no. 4). Ithaca, N.Y.: Society for Applied Anthropology.

Carrithers, Michael, Steven Collins, and Steven Lukes (eds) (1985). *The Category of the Person: Anthropology, Philosophy, History*. Cambridge: Cambridge University Press. (This volume contains a translation of Marcel Mauss's essay 'A Category of the Human Mind: The notion of Person, the Notion of Self', and comments on the subject by several eminent anthropologists, including Louis Dumont.)

Carsten, Janet (1995). 'The Substance of Kinship and the Heat of the Hearth: Feeding, Personhood and Relatedness among Malays in Pulau Langkawi'. *American Ethnologist* 22(2): 223–41.

Conklin, Beth A, and Lynne M. Morgan (1996). 'Babies, Bodies, and the Production of Personhood in North America and a Native Amazonian Society'. *Ethos* 24(4): 657–94.

De Waal, Frans (2000). *Chimpanzee Politics: Power and Sex among Apes.* Baltimore, Md.: Johns Hopkins University Press.

Goffman, Erving (1959). *The Presentation of Self in Everyday Life.* London: Penguin Books.

Pasternak, Charles (ed.) (2007). *What Makes Us Human?* Oxford: Oneworld Publications.

Stringer, Christopher (2006) *Homo Britannicus: The Incredible Story of Human Life in Britain.* London: Allen Lane.

6 Ritual, ceremony, and identity

Ardener, Edwin (1972). 'Belief and the Problem of Women' in J. S. La Fontaine (ed.). *The Interpretation of Ritual: Essays in Honour of A. I. Richards.* London: Tavistock Publications.

Ardener, Shirley (1981). *Women and Space: Ground Rules and Social Maps.* New York: St. Martin's Press.

Ben-Nathan, Geoffrey (2008). *"I'm Adult, Aren't I!": Understanding Juvenile Delinquency and Creating Adults Out of Children – The Case for a Formal Rite of Passage.* Jerusalem: Rubin Mass.

Bourdieu, Pierre (2003). 'The Berber House' in Setha M. Low and Denise Lawrence-Zúñiga (eds.). *The Anthropology of Space and Place: Locating Culture.* Malden, Mass.: Blackwell Publications.

Diamant, Anita (2002). *The Red Tent.* Basingstoke, UK: Pan Macmillan.

La Fontaine, J. S. (1985). *Initiation,* Harmondsworth: Penguin.

Matthews, Gordon (2000). *Global Culture/Individual Identity: Searching for Home in the Cultural Supermarket.* London and New York: Routledge.

Mernissi, Fatima (2011). *Beyond the Veil: Male-Female Dynamics in Modern Muslim Society*. London: Saqi Book Publishers.

Ogasawara, Yuko (1998). *Office Ladies and Salaried Men: Power, Gender and Work in Japanese Companies*. Berkeley: University of California Press.

Okely, Judith (1996). 'Gypsy Women: Models in Conflict' in J. Okely (ed.). *Own or Other Culture*. London: Routledge.

Van Gennep, Arnold (1960). *The Rites of Passage*. London: Routledge & Kegan Paul.

Turner, Victor (1967). *The Forest of Symbols: Aspects of Ndembu Ritual*. Cornell, N.Y.: Cornell University Press.

7 Ways of belonging

Ardener Shirley (ed.) (1981). *Women and Space: Ground Rules and Social Maps*. London: Croom Helm.

Bachnik, Jane M. (1998). 'Time, Space and Person in Japanese Relationships' in Joy Hendry (ed.). *Interpreting Japanese Society: Anthropological Approaches*. London: Routledge.

Bourdieu, Pierre. (1990). 'The Kabyle House or the World Reversed' in *The Logic of Practice*. Cambridge, UK: Polity Press.

Carsten, Janet, and Stephen Hugh-Jones (1995). *About the House: Lévi-Strauss and Beyond*. Cambridge: Cambridge University Press.

Eliade, Mircea (1964). *Shamanism: Archaic Techniques of Ecstasy*. Princeton: Princeton University Press.

Evans-Pritchard, E. E. (1940). *The Nuer: A Description of the Modes of Livelihood and Political Institutions of a Nilotic People*. Oxford: Clarendon Press.

Fox, James J. (1993). *Inside Austronesian Houses: Perspectives on Domestic Designs for Living*. Canberra: Australian National University Press.

Knight, John (2000). *Natural Enemies: People-Wildlife Conflicts in Anthropological Perspective*. London and New York: Routledge.

Lock, Margaret (2002). *Twice Dead: Organ Transplants and the Reinvention of Death*. Berkeley: University of California Press.

Watson, C.W. (1997). 'Born a Lady, Became a Princess, Died a Saint: The Reaction to the Death of Diana, Princess of Wales'. *Anthropology Today* 13(6): 3–7.

8 The global species

Appadurai, Arjun (ed.) (1988). *The Social Life of Things: Commodities in Cultural Perspective*. Cambridge: Cambridge University Press.

Bicker, Alan, Paul Sillitoe, and Johan Pottier (2004). *Development and Local Knowledge*. London and New York: Routledge.

Douglas, Mary, and Baron Isherwood (eds) (1996). *The World of Goods: Towards an Anthropology of Consumption*. London and New York: Routledge.

Finlayson, Clive (2010). *The Humans Who Went Extinct: Why Neanderthals Died Out And We Survived*. Oxford: Oxford University Press.

Hendry, Joy (2000). *The Orient Strikes Back: A Global View of Cultural Display*. Oxford: Berg Publishers.

Howes, David (1996). *Cross-Cultural Consumption: Global Markets, Local Realities*. London and New York: Routledge.

Inda, Jonathan Xavier, and Renato Rosaldo (eds) (2002). *The Anthropology of Globalisation: A Reader*. Oxford: Blackwell.

Kapferer, Bruce (ed.) (2004). *The World Trade Center and Global Crisis: Critical Perspective*. New York and Oxford: Berghahn Books.

Lewin, Roger, and Robert Andrew Foley (2004). *Principles of Human Evolution*. Oxford: Blackwell.

Mintz, Sidney Wilfred (1985). *Sweetness and Power: The Place of Sugar in Modern History*. New York: Viking.

Sahlins, Marshall (1988). 'Cosmologies of Capitalism: The Trans-Pacific Sector of "The World System"' (Radcliffe-Brown Lecture in Social Anthropology). *Proceedings of the British Academy* 74: 1–51.

Sillitoe, Paul, Alan Bicker, and Johan Pottier (eds) (2001). *Participating in Development: Approaches to Indigenous Knowledge.* London and New York: Routledge.

Stanley, Nick (1998). *Being Ourselves for You: The Global Display of Cultures.* London: Middlesex University Press.

Stringer, Chris (2011). *The Origin of Our Species.* London: Allen Lane.

Watson, James L. (ed.) (1998). *Golden Arches East: McDonalds in East Asia.* Stanford, Calif.: Stanford University Press.

Wilk, Richard (2006). *Home Cooking in the Global Village: Caribbean Food from Buccaneers to Ecotourists.* Oxford and New York: Berg Publishers.

Wood, Bernard (2005). *Human Evolution: A Very Short Introduction.* Oxford: Oxford University Press.

Wrangham, Richard (2009). *Catching Fire: How Cooking Made Us Human.* London: Profile Books.

9 Anthropology in the age of global communication

Abram, Simone (1997). 'Performing for Tourists in Rural France' in Simone Abram, Jacqueline Waldren, and Donald V. L. Macleod (eds). *Tourists and Tourism: Identifying with People and Places.* Oxford and New York: Berg Publishers.

Chatty, Dawn, and Marcus Colchester (eds) (2002). *Conservation and Mobile Indigenous Peoples: Displacement, Forced Settlement and Sustainable Development.* Oxford and New York: Berghahn Books.

Eriksen, Thomas Hylland (ed.) (2003). *Globalisation: Studies in Anthropology.* London and Sterling, Va.: Pluto Press.

Hannerz, Ulf (1996). *Transnational Connections: Culture, People, Places.* London and New York: Routledge.

Hendry, Joy (2005). *Reclaiming Culture: Indigenous Peoples and Self-Representation.* New York: Palgrave.

Hirschon, Renee (1989). *Heirs of the Greek Catastrophe: The Social Life of Asia Minor Refugees in Piraeus.* Oxford: Clarendon Press.

Johnston, Alison (2006). *Is the Sacred for Sale?: Tourism and Indigenous Peoples*. London: Earthscan.

Shaw, Alison (2000). *Kinship and Continuity: Pakistani Families in Britain*. London: Routledge.

Landzelius, Kyra (2006). *Native on the Net: Indigenous and Diasporic Peoples in the Virtual Age*. London and New York: Routledge.

Miller, Daniel, and Don Slater (2000). *The Internet: An Ethnographic Approach*. Oxford: Berg Publishers.

Smith, Valene L., and Maryann Brent (eds) (2001). *Hosts and Guests Revisited: Tourism Issues of the 21st Century*. New York: Cognizant Communication Corp.

Wulff, Helena (2001). *Ballet Across Borders: Career and Culture in the World of Dancers*. Oxford and New York: Berg Publishers.

Yamashita, Shinji (2003). *Bali and Beyond: Explorations in the Anthropology of Tourism,* trans. by J. S. Eades. Oxford and New York: Berghahn Books.

10 Practising anthropology

American Anthropological Society, 'Professional Ethics' (http://www.aaanet.org/profdev/ethics/) and the Association of Social Anthropologists of the UK and Commonwealth, 'Ethical Guidelines for Good Research Practice' (http://www.theasa.org/ethics/guidelines.shtml).

Bloch, Maurice (2005). 'Where Did Anthropology Go?: Or the Need for "Human Nature"' in Maurice Bloch (ed.). *Essays on Cultural Transmission* (LSE Monographs on Social Anthropology). Oxford: Berg Publishers.

Davies, Charlotte Aull (2008). *Reflexive Ethnography: A Guide to Researching Selves and Others*. London and New York: Routledge.

Eriksen, Thomas Hylland (2006). *Engaging Anthropology: The Case for a Public Presence*. Oxford and New York: Berg Publishers.

Evans, Grant (1993). *Asia's Cultural Mosaic: An Anthropological Introduction*. New York: Prentice Hall.

Hendry, Joy (1993). *Wrapping Culture: Politeness and Presentation in Japan and Other Societies*. Oxford: Clarendon Press.

Okely, Judith, and Helen Callaway (eds) (1992). *Anthropology and Autobiography*. London and New York: Routledge.

Ribeiro, Gustavo Lins, and Arturo Escobar (2006). *World Anthropologies: Disciplinary Transformations within Systems of Power*. Oxford and New York: Berg Publishers.

Tuhiwai Smith, Linda (1999). *Decolonizing Methodologies: Research and Indigenous Peoples*. Dunedin, N.Z.: University of Otago Press.

Wilson, Richard Ashby, and Jon P. Mitchell (2003). *Human Rights in Global Perspective: Anthropological Studies of Rights, Claims and Entitlements*. London: Routledge.

Index